Black Students and Higher Education

SRHE and Open University Press Imprint
General Editor: Heather Eggins

Black Students and Higher Education

John Bird

The Society for Research into Higher Education
& Open University Press

Published by SRHE and
Open University Press
Celtic Court
22 Ballmoor
Buckingham
MK18 1XW

and 1900 Frost Road, Suite 101
Bristol, PA 19007, USA

First Published 1996

A catalogue record of this book is available from the British Library

ISBN   0 335 19626 8 (pb)   0 335 19627 6 (hb)

Library of Congress Cataloging-in-Publication Data
Francis, John, 1944–
    Black students and higher education : rhetorics and realities /
John F. Bird.
        p. cm.
    Includes bibliographical references and index.
    ISBN 0-335-19627-6 (hc). — ISBN 0-335-19626-8 (pbk.)
    1. Blacks—Education (Higher)—Great Britain. 2. College
students, Black—Great Britain. I. Title.
    LC2806.G7F73   1996
    378.1′98′296041—dc20   96–12068
                                                                CIP

Typeset by Graphicraft Typesetters Ltd, Hong Kong
Printed in Great Britain by St Edmundsbury Press Ltd, Bury St Edmunds, Suffolk

Contents

Preface

What follows is a study of access to higher education (HE) for black students and their progression through HE and into employment. This is based on a limited amount of existing work, complemented by two pieces of research carried out for the Employment Department between 1989 and 1992: a study in a group of schools and higher education institutions (HEIs) in the Bath and Bristol areas; and a study of ethnic monitoring in HEIs in England. There is a focus on the analysis of barriers to access to HE and progression within HE facing black students, but also an emphasis on developing practices which attempt to enhance access and progression, including comprehensive systems of ethnic monitoring.

While it is recognized that different ethnic minority groups have different experiences of access and progression, there is frequently a common experience of racial discrimination. Indeed, people who racially discriminate in overt – and often covert – fashion usually make no distinction between different minorities; they, as it were, discriminate indiscriminately. It is for this reason – and because the overwhelming majority of students in the Bath and Bristol study wanted this – that the term 'black' is frequently used below. This is not to deny the political issues involved in using this term to refer to a range of ethnic minority groups. In acceding to what most of the interviewees wanted, we have not followed Cole's (1993: 673) injunction to sociologists and other researchers to use the term 'Asian, black and other minority ethnic'. There is good reason to use 'minority ethnic', in that the alternative, 'ethnic minority', disguises the fact that both majorities and minorities have ethnicities. However, possible debates about the meaning of Asian and black, and about which should come first in any nomenclature, will not be pursued here. There is a significant point, for example, in Modood's (1994) argument that in referring to Asians as black we may significantly underplay the cultural antipathy which Asian people face, a cultural antipathy which is greater, for him, than that faced by people of Afro-Caribbean origin. Less convincing is Modood's suggestion that using the term black is somehow old-fashioned and makes it difficult to discuss the variety of new ethnicities. There needs to be some middle position between two extremes: that which involves an assertion that each ethnicity is distinct and that which claims that all minorities have something in common.

There is, considering the increase in the numbers of black students entering HE, surprisingly little work which deals with their experiences. There is even less that looks at barriers to successful progression and strategies to enhance the quality of the student experience. This is one of the reasons why, in what follows, there is a good deal of reference to work developed in further education (FE) and to a lesser extent in schools. HE has much to learn from work done in FE (for example, by the Further Education Unit and Unit for the Development of Adult and Continuing Education), work which, as far as most HE staff are concerned, has received little if any attention. There seems to be little mileage in an argument that the experience of FE and schools in dealing with diversity is only relevant to those sectors. A willingness to learn from FE and school experience will also avoid any need for HEIs to reinvent policy and practice.

Quotations from named students and from staff in Chapters 2–6 are taken from Bird *et al.* (1992a, b) or from previously unpublished interview transcripts.

Introduction

The theme of what follows is the experience of black students seeking entry to higher education institutions and what happens to them when they gain entry. The concern is with the quality of the educational experience of those students, and how what has been called equality assurance can be developed and maintained (Runnymede Trust, 1993). HEIs have been successful in recruiting increasing numbers of black students. For example, data from back to 1991, when the admissions systems for the then polytechnics and universities started monitoring applications and acceptances for degrees by ethnicity, indicate that black acceptances have been significant and increasing: from some 8.5 per cent in 1991–2 to some 9.8 per cent in 1993–4 (UCCA, 1992; UCAS, 1994, 1995). There are, however, clear barriers to *access* to HE and barriers to successful *progression* once entry is gained, and a small but significant body of work identifies these barriers while focusing mainly on issues of access.[1] This body of work provides the grounding for what follows; that is, a study of barriers to access and progression and of strategies which can be used to enhance the quality of provision for black people. As such, the aim is to recognize the success of black students in entering and succeeding in HE, but also to emphasize the background of difficulties and impediments which face many of them.

Access and progression

The barriers facing black students are numerous: lack of relevant information on post-16 education; discouragement from thinking about HE; isolation once in HE; lack of black staff in HE; discrimination by staff and students in HE; unresponsive curriculum responses to ethnic diversity in HE. In part, the idea behind much of what follows is not only to provide an analysis of barriers but also to suggest some strategies which staff and students in schools and HE can use. It is important to emphasize here that any strategies to deal with access and progression must be available for staff *and* students. Not only are there likely to be strategies which are specific to staff (curriculum development, for example) and to students (the development of support groups may be a case in point here), but also, where black students do face discrimination, they experience it as arising from interactions with both staff and students.

What follows is informed by a deep conviction that discrimination is both harmful and wasteful, and that it often happens without people being aware of it. There is also a somewhat liberal tone to this work: much can be done *within* existing structures even when reasons will be given for not doing anything, reasons that, as we will see, are often related to resource constraints. It may, of course, turn out that not everything that needs to be done can be accomplished without radical changes in institutional practice, including in those institutions beyond the education system; that higher education cannot, in that sense, compensate for a society in which there is widespread discrimination. Part of the difficulty is, of course, that the problems faced by black students are often not recognized and therefore nothing is done. In addition to a lack of recognition of these problems there are, as we will see below, tendencies to say that black students exaggerate their problems and/ or that the problems they face are related exclusively to their own cultural values and attitudes.

The tenor of this work is set in the title of Chapter 1, 'Rhetorics of access and realities of exclusion'; in other words, access to HE is not an end in itself if the experience of black students, once there, is an alienating one. As such, this chapter seeks to identify the barriers to access and full participation in HE for a range of ethnic minority groups, in particular Afro-Caribbean and Asian groups, seeking and gaining entry, and to study their experiences of HE. These barriers are also discussed within the context of the policy debate about positive action and the extent to which – maliciously or otherwise – this is confused with positive discrimination. In addition, this work is located within the debate about race research, including the politics and ethics of such research.

Part 1 identifies a number of strategies which can be developed with schools and with parents. In Chapter 2, the focus on black students in schools is deliberately a focus on mainstream provision and does not, therefore, discuss provision for mature black people. This is largely because such provision, including access courses, has been well analysed elsewhere (FEU, 1986b, d, 1987b). These analyses suggest that dedicated black access courses are an effective way of increasing mature black access to higher education. Strategies for involving black students in work with school students is described and evaluated. In addition, the development of more comprehensive frameworks for collaboration between HE, schools and colleges is discussed. Chapter 3 looks at strategies for increasing the flow of quality information which is going to black people, both as parents and as potential HE students.

Part 2 concerns those black students who do enter HE and focuses on improving the quality of their experiences. In Chapter 4, the establishment of staff and curriculum development work with respect to ethnic diversity is considered as a crucial element of quality assurance in HE. Chapter 5 investigates strategies which involve black students developing their own support groups in HE, where they are usually in a marked minority. The focus of Part 3 is on monitoring and subsequent progression from HE. How can HEIs know what is happening to black students? This knowledge is a precondition for policy formation and could and should come to play a crucial role in HE teaching quality assessment; it is a body of knowledge which will need to include quantitative and qualitative information about on-course experiences and what happens to black students when they leave HE. At the ends of Chapters 3 to 6 there are sections which take up some of the central theoretical and conceptual issues in the study of race and education.

Race and research

There is considerable debate and controversy concerning race-related research (see, for example, Foster, 1990; Leicester and Taylor, 1992). This controversy raises a range of ethical and political issues, in particular, whether race-related research should be occurring, who funds such research, who should be carrying it out, and the uses to which such research is put. The question about whether such research should be taking place relates, in part, to the history of race research and to a certain resistance to the regularity with which black communities are subject to research activity. Williams (1988: 136), referring to research on the youth services, puts it nicely: 'Gus John relates the resentment which black people felt towards his research team: "We were brought face to face with the anger and frustration of black people in England at being the subject of even more surveys, researches, studies and reports".'

To take the Bath and Bristol research as an example, while these ethical and political issues might have remained in some ways unresolved, the design and implementation did expressly address them. First, the work was discussed widely with black organizations and there was no general opposition to the work. There was a healthy scepticism over why the research was happening and how black people would benefit. In part, this related to previous attempts to open up further education provision to black people, which were seen as less than positive, and to a concern that black people had already been the recipients of frequent analyses of their education needs. The worry was, in part, that such needs analyses had produced few positive outcomes and therefore that further attempts to assess need might have the same results.

Second, one member of the project team, who subsequently became project coordinator, was black, which proved crucial when interviewees were talking of discrimination and powerlessness. Third, the results of the research were fed back to those black people involved in the work and came to inform institutional practices in some of the HEIs involved. Fourth, a steering group which managed the project included representatives from a wide range of interests, and a majority black membership, thus acting to moderate any domination by the funder, the Employment Department. Finally, reproduction of stereotypes of black people was avoided, in particular the use of ideas and approaches which emphasize either that black people have self-generated deficits which need to be corrected or that aspects of their culture play a central and determining role in educational underachievement. If there are underachievements and deficits then we should seek the origins of these, and the solutions to them, in the interactions between groups – black and white – in social structures where there are differentials of power.

Perhaps the most important issue for this work was the involvement of a black interviewer/coordinator. Rhodes (1994) has argued that 'racial' matching of interviewer and respondent serves, among other things, to marginalize black people in the academic hierarchy and may be done simply to legitimate research work with black people. While we agree with Rhodes that 'race', like gender, is a contextual feature of all social research, irrespective of the 'race' or gender of its subjects (Rhodes, 1994: 558), racial matching of interviewer and interviewee seems to be a minor reason why black academics are often employed in the lower reaches of academic work. That black people are employed simply to give legitimacy to research is, again, questionable in that it suggests that black communities would not be aware of this and would, as it were, be duped into supporting such work simply because of the presence of a black interviewer. There can, in fact, be considerable advantages in using a black interviewer, including the provision of a supportive environment in which sensitive and difficult issues could be discussed. Part of an institutional positive action strategy would then involve ensuring that successful black researchers have a career path that neither keeps them doing research nor restricts them to race-related research.

There is, of course, no *necessary* link between the good reasons for using black interviewees and those arguments which press for the exclusion of white researchers from race research. All social science research is probably best done by teams, and that would apply to race research. The important point is to have teams that contain black people but without necessarily excluding white people; such exclusion will, of course, sometimes be appropriate, including in situations where black people desire such an exclusion. The structure of such teams will, in large measure, relate to the aims and objectives of the work concerned. However, the effectiveness of teams will largely be determined by the value given to each member's work and the extent to which that work relates to their knowledge and expertise. It is on this latter point that problems can arise where well-qualified black people are given routine duties even when they are as well or better qualified than their white colleagues. Dealing with these issues is the point of any positive action strategies which need to guide the formation of research teams.

As Westwood (1992) indicates – and as is the case with at least some of the research concerning black students' access and progression – what is important is the transformative capacity of race-related work; what, in such research, links what Mills (1970) defines as private troubles and public issues. Especially when dealing with race research, we are in a contested and highly politicized domain; part of the transformative effect is the political empowerment of those involved. As Westwood puts it in describing a particular piece of research, 'The research has, therefore, become an important political tool in which knowledge and experiences which were private pains have become a collective document, collectively produced and owned' (Westwood, 1992: 197).

A key element in the research process is why interviewees want to be interviewed. The motivations of the Bath and Bristol students are best summed up in the following quotation from Westwood (1992: 196): 'I am talking to you because I want to be heard.' Many of Westwood's interviewees and many of those in the Bath and Bristol study saw the interview process as therapeutic. It is both a strength and a weakness of this work that it is therapeutic, or at least can become similar to a therapeutic environment. The strength is that people can talk about their painful experiences; the weakness that the interviewer(s) will not have therapeutic skills and should not attempt to become a therapist. It is, of course, still an interesting point that, for many black students, the research environment *is* the one in which issues of race and discrimination are first being discussed. In part, the reason is to do with the absence of any other forum for such discussions in many HEIs and the relative ineffectiveness of those structures established to deal with racial harassment.

We have some reservations over Westwood's (1992: 195) idea that transformative research should not take subjects as cases. There seems to be an issue here of what we mean by a *case* and whether, for example, it is legitimate to use interview data to indicate what we might call ideal typical situations facing black students.

On ethnography

Despite a small number of works addressing black students in HE, there is little which looks at their experiences in detail and which then seeks to develop strategies that tackle the variety of barriers to entry and progression. There is, in other words, a noisy silence about black students and no codification of their experiences. Part of the silence may be based upon the idea that the liberal academy is not a site of discrimination. Another part may follow from the idea that existing structures, such as codes of practice on racial abuse and harassment, are working. A final part may follow from the belief that where there are complaints of discrimination they are ill-founded or exaggerated.

There is an increasing recognition in social sciences of the value of ethnography, particularly in gaining access to the perceptions that people have of their social positions and locations. In this sense, the Bristol and Bath research was ethnographic and included interviews with 105 black, predominantly Afro-Caribbean and Asian students, and a small number of white students, in five schools and three HEIs in the area. Hour long, unstructured interviews were recorded, with respondents' permission, and then transcribed. Transcriptions were coded using a modified version of ETHNOGRAPH in order to facilitate final analysis. The outcome is what might be called narratives of the self, which provide rich insights into the educational histories and aspirations of black students and ideas on how such educational provision might be improved. It is important to be aware of both the nature and the limitations of ethnographic research and the advantages of triangulation (see Chapter 6 below; see also Atkinson, 1990; Hammersley, 1992; Silverman, 1993; Jordan and Yeomans, 1995). We can characterize ethnography as a qualitative method, frequently including semi- or unstructured interviews. It is usually boundary work in that it involves looking at 'other' ways of life and behaving, with all the possibilities of mis- understanding and pathologization that this entails. This is especially acute when one is looking at issues of ethnicity, where there is often a boundary between researcher and subject which reproduces already existing social boundaries; that is, those of discrimination and prejudice. There is there- fore a need for a critical ethnography which is aware of the positioning of researchers and those they study, and which is, therefore, reflexive. The point of such reflexivity is to challenge common assumptions about the nature of social science research. As Jordan and Yeomans (1995: 394) put it, 'Reflexivity represents ethnography's attempt to resolve the dualisms of contemporary social theory, i.e. object/subject, theory/practice, action/struc- ture and so on.' Put another way, such research is part of the everyday world as well as being constitutive of it.

In practice, therefore, ethnography requires not only the more obvious things – careful design of interview schedules, sensitivity in delivering them, care in interpretation – but also a deeper awareness that the researcher operates in a political situation and that his or her work may, at best, be misunderstood or, at worst, subverted. Equally, the ethnographer must develop ways of approaching and involving the subject of interviews that is not disempowering and does not take the results of research totally out of the hands of subjects. In others words, critical ethnography seeks to make the subject of interviews much more than a subject.

It is crucial to stress that what has been achieved here could not have been achieved without some valuable existing work (see note 1), but espe- cially without the considerable support and openness of the black inter- viewees in Bath and Bristol. That openness contrasts with the resistance to research identified by Williams (1988).

A note on race, racism and racialism

Although this is not the place to debate, in full, the terms race, racism and racism, there is a number of important issues which provide a background to some of the discussion below. These issues include what we mean by race and racism; how far race is seen to constitute the totality of black experience; and the debate about what has been termed ethnic essentialism (Gilroy, 1993).

The terminology is reasonably easy to clarify. Race refers either to imputed, but fictive, biological differences between groups which are seen, in one way or another, to determine how those groups behave, or to cultural differences between social groups which are real and become the basis for discrimination. This latter, culturalist, emphasis has been called, by Barker (1981), the new racism. Racism then becomes the discriminatory structures based upon the biological and cultural differences. Racialism is, then, that series of attitudes which are prejudicial, and which are often manifested within discriminatory structures. The difference between race and ethnicity here is not only a difference between biological and cultural differences, but also one between the empirical emptiness and falsity of racial categories and the reality of ethnic differences. Crucially, the reality of ethnic differences is itself complex. Such cultural differences include not only what people within those cultures recognize and accept, but also misunderstandings and distortions of those cultures by others who do not have allegiances to them.

Three issues follow from this attempt at definition. As Mason (1994: 847) suggests, what we call biological racism was always more than that, for it included how these biological categories determined personal, social and cultural competencies. The important thing about biological racism was, therefore, not only its biological components but that these became the basis for structural and symbolic acts of exclusion. Second, as Gilroy argues, there is a major danger in reducing the totality of black experiences to racism: '[we] must not . . . reduce the complexity of black life to an effect of racism' (Gilroy, 1987: 150). For Gilroy this not only leads us to neglect other aspects of the lives of black people but portrays them as passive victims of a racism 'sweeping all before it' (Gilroy, 1987: 150). This view is put in a slightly different way by Miles (1989), who identifies a conceptual inflation of the term race to include such a wide variety of cultural phenomena as to empty the term of much of its explanatory value. As Miles puts it,

> By widening the definition [of racism] to include any deterministic attribution of qualities to a group identified as biologically or culturally distinct . . . it therefore includes arguments such as 'Women should not be put in positions of responsibility because their emotional character prevents them from making rational decisions' and 'I don't go to Italian restaurants because Italians are rude'. It therefore becomes impossible to differentiate arguments which, as in the former example, might otherwise be designated as sexist.
>
> (Miles, 1989: 50)

Finally there is the argument developed in, for example, Gilroy's later work (1993), that we should reject all essentialist approaches to race; that is, all approaches which attempt to identify an essence of race that is transhistorical and immutable. The point is not only that race is lived and resisted, but that all attempts to define the essence of a group, for example, a culture (British, Irish, Afro-Caribbean), reveal these to be hybrids. As Gilroy (1993: xi) put it, 'There are two aspirations that I would like to share with readers . . . The first is my hope that the contents of this book are unified by a concern to refute the dangerous obsession with "racial" purity . . . It is, after all, an essay about . . . inescapable hybridity.' And again: 'An additional, and possibly more profound, area of political difficulty comes into view [with] the voguish language of absolute ethnic difference' (Gilroy, 1993: 34).

This short section is merely meant to show how contested is the language with which we describe different groups, and how politicized the whole debate about race. As such, it would be surprising if the relationships between issues of race, ethnicity and education were any the less contested and politicized. The academic world has not, itself, made race issues any the less difficult to deal with. It is noticeable that within the academy, processes which Gillborn and others refer to as deracialization are at work. As we will see, these processes include not only trying to reduce race to something else – social class, for example – but also to seeing race issues as really issues of prejudice. In academic discourse, this process has occurred in the more or less total disappearance of the term race, its frequent appearance in inverted commas – as if to suggests that it is not really the right word to use – and its replacement by 'ethnicity' and 'ethnic antagonism'.

Note

1 Some of the most useful works here include Craft and Craft (1983), Tomlinson (1983), Brienberg (1987), Lyon (1988), Sammons and Newbury (1989), Williams *et al.* (1989), Singh (1990), Jewson *et al.* (1991), Allan (1992), Bird *et al.* (1992b, c), Leicester and Taylor (1992), Taylor (1992), Leicester (1993a, b), Connolly (1994), Modood and Shiner (1994), Moodley (1995) and Kibble (n.d.).

1

Rhetorics of Access and Realities of Exclusion

[The] greatest danger lies in the possibility that ill-conceived and poorly-formulated studies will perpetuate the notion of black educational underachievement as a given rather than as a problematic that requires sensitive and systematic interrogation.

(Troyna, 1984: 164)

University was not even mentioned, nobody thought I would go there, that was the general attitude of the whole school ... I actually remember my careers teacher laughing at me when I said I was applying for university and she actually told me to forget it ... it was a 3 minute conversation.

(Michael, Afro-Caribbean interviewee)

I don't see any black or Asian lecturers ... if there was a black or Asian lecturer, how would he be received by all the white students ... I think the way things are they would not be received well.

(Shaffique, Asian interviewee)

There is a widespread recognition that access to higher education is something which should be widened, in particular to include groups who have not – in the recent past – successfully entered such institutions. The justifications for this are varied. Wider access is commonly related to equitable treatment, to treating people on their merits and to the costs, including legal ones, of not treating people equitably. The desire for equity also often includes a commitment to serving the needs of communities and the needs of individuals in those communities. Increasingly, for many HEIs those communities are local ones, in large measure because of the financial costs for students of studying away from their localities. Finally, equity is often linked to economic efficiency, in that wasting people's talents includes wasting their potential to contribute to economic prosperity. This commitment to access and equity is part of the missions of all HEIs and it is now extremely unlikely that staff in any HEI would say otherwise. Commitments to access for all students who might benefit are as central to the public face of HEIs as are commitments to equal opportunities policies in staff recruitment.

Perhaps the major theme of this work is that – if we consider access and progression together, and recognize that opening the doors of HE is only a small part of the process – we cannot take the rhetoric about access and the quality of the black student experience as necessarily what is happening in reality. As Brienberg (1987) suggests, black and white people even have different perspectives on this whole issue; whereas white people emphasize issues of access, black people are far more concerned with what happens when black students enter HE. In this context, and despite the widely held support for access from government, funding councils, access practitioners and groups representing black people, we find that the experience of black students in HE is frequently not characterized by quality treatment or by equality of treatment. In addition, we find that the predominantly white staff and students in HEIs often do not know what it is like being a black student, at least in part because of inadequate systems of monitoring. The lessons that need to be learned are indicated in the following: 'For too long HE has been the victim of its own ideology. Discrimination has been rendered invisible by a liberal ethos that makes it difficult even to discuss the possibility of unequal treatment' (Dorn, 1991).

This draws us to the heart of the debate and towards the heart of this book. If the doors are open, is that a sufficient condition for arguing that HE is meeting the needs of black students? If not, then what are the internal barriers to success for black students and how might they be tackled? More widely, do successful black students have success when they leave university and enter the labour market?

The issue of wider access for black students is one which, although receiving tacit support, has been contested in a number of ways. One of the most common uses the language of positive discrimination to imply two things: that there is not, in fact, a problem of black access to HE, so that what is done by HEIs must be discrimination and special treatment; and, relatedly, that strategies which do widen access do so by lowering standards of entry for black students. The fact that positive discrimination is legally impermissible, and although there is no evidence of systematic lowering of entry requirements, has not stopped the confusion of what is illegal – positive discrimination – and what is allowed – positive action. This confusion has been characteristic of media discussions of admissions data which suggest that black people do well in entry to higher education. For example, the *Times Higher Education Supplement* of 19 January 1991, in a report headed 'Poly targets minority groups', argued that an institution practised positive discrimination through its targeting. As we shall see, positive action and positive discrimination are distinct, and there is no necessary link between setting targets, commonly associated with the former, and establishing quotas, usually linked with positive discrimination. The complexities of these issues can be indicated if we look at two related issues here: figures on admission to HE for black people and how these might relate to positive action strategies.

Access and admissions figures

It is important to have a picture of the ethnic minority populations in the UK as background to what follows. The overall picture for the population of

Table 1.1 Population: 1991 Census

	Percentage in population
White	94.5
Black Caribbean	0.9
Black African	0.4
Indian	1.5
Pakistani	0.9
Bangladeshi	0.3
Chinese	0.3

Source: OPCS Decennial Census, 1991.

Table 1.2 Cumulative distribution, by age and ethnicity, 1988–90 (percentages)

	White	*All ethnic minorities*	*Afro-Caribbean*	*Pakistani*	*Indian*	*Bangladeshi*	*Chinese*
Under 10	12	23	24	29	18	25	17
Under 20	25	42	38	54	37	56	33
Under 30	41	61	59	69	54	72	54

Source: Based on Jones, 1993: 23.

Table 1.3 Ethnicity and qualifications (percentage of population with qualification)

	White	*Afro-Caribbean*	*Southern Asian*[a]
Four or more GCSE/O levels	31	18	39
NVQ 1/2	28	34	27

[a] Southern Asian includes Bangladeshi, Indian and Pakistani.
Source: Based on Jones, 1993: 37.

the UK from the 1991 Census indicates that ethnic minorities make up 4.3 per cent of the population (Owen, 1992). The largest minority population is those of Indian origin, who constitute a fifth of the total. The population of Afro-Caribbean origin is the only one to have declined, and the fastest rate of growth is in those of Bangladeshi and African origin. An extract from the 1991 Census is shown in Table 1.1.

Residentially, this population is urban, with 44.8 per cent living in London, which has 10 per cent of the white population (Owen, 1992: 2, 3). This population also has a distinct age profile, indicated in cumulative percentages in Table 1.2.

In terms of qualifications, there are important patterns indicated, for example, in those aged 16–19 with four or more GCSE/O levels and those with vocational qualifications (see Table 1.3).

Two additional things are important. First, those of Indian origin are more qualified than those of Pakistani and Bangladeshi origin. Second, although ethnic minorities are more likely to stay in education post-16 than whites, significant proportions do so in order to take or resit GCSEs, and are therefore likely to take A levels when older than white students. For those aged 25–44, the qualification structure is also diverse. Those of Pakistani and Bangladeshi origin are least qualified, in particular women, 70 per cent of whom lack any recognized and accredited qualifications; men of African, Chinese, Indian and African Asian origin are more likely to have degrees than white men; Afro-Caribbean and African women are better qualified than women in other minority ethnic groups. The size, urban concentration, age structure and qualifications profile have, as we will see, important implications for strategies for access to HE and progression through HE.

There is some evidence from annual admissions data that black students do well in entry to HE compared with their white peers. For example, for 1990–1 entry to the then polytechnics and colleges of HE, 10 per cent of admissions were Asian and 4.5 per cent were black; this compared with 5.4 and 1 per cent respectively for the then university sector (see Bird *et al.*, 1992b). Subsequent years have seen a slow but steady increase in the numbers of black students accepted for HE; for 1993–4, acceptances for degrees were at 9.8 per cent for the sector, with Indian and Chinese students doing as well as or better than white students, and Bangladeshi, Pakistani and Afro-Caribbean men doing less well than their white counterparts (UCAS, 1995). As Modood and Shiner (1994: especially 43–51) indicate, there is a divide between the former polytechnics and colleges, which do best in accessing Afro-Caribbean and Indian applicants, and the traditional universities, which are more likely to access Chinese and some other groups of Asian students. Put negatively, Chinese and Bangladeshi students are less likely to gain entry to the former polytechnics and colleges, while Afro-Caribbean and Pakistani students are less likely to enter the traditional universities. It was this data on the increasing success of black students that was often described as constituting evidence that HEIs were operating policies of positive discrimination.

On average, or so it would seem, black and Asian students enter HEIs in greater numbers than their representation in the population would indicate, with specific groups of Chinese and Asian students doing particularly well. There is a deliberate scepticism in the last sentence, which relates to how we conceptualize under-representation. This sceptical emphasis is important for a number of reasons. First, when we look at the structure of ethnic minority populations in the context of general census data (Coleman and Salt, 1992; Owen, 1992; Jones, 1993), there is no simple sense in which we can decide on who is underrepresented. To take the example of age structures, we have seen that ethnic minority populations are generally younger than the white population. As such, there is actually a large number passing through schools and, hence, a potentially large population demanding access to HE. Second, sector-wide figures disguise the fact that black students are concentrated in a small number of HEIs. Modood (1993), for example, indicates that in five of the ex-polytechnics 40 per cent of students are black. In many institutions, therefore, there are very small proportions of black students indeed, with resulting problems of isolation and possible discrimination, which are discussed later. Seen another way, a small number of institutions seems to be doing the majority of the redressing of past imbalances in participation, and these are predominantly ex-polytechnics.

Third, the classifications of ethnic groups which form the basis of the statistical exercise are themselves racialized, in that they stress ethnic origin, which may have little meaning for black students who have lived in Britain for their whole lives. This may be important in increasing the likelihood that students will not complete forms which ask for details of ethnicity because the meanings of 'Asian', 'Black African' and so on will be unclear. While this may not be so important for purposes of ethnic statistics it might be important for developing policies to respond to ethnic diversity in HE. In essence, then, the interpretation of the statistics is a complex matter, itself replete with political implications. While the statistics do represent success for many black students, they cannot be taken at face value as an indicator that HEIs have achieved their missions. Nor should they be isolated from what happens to black people who leave HE and enter the labour market, where, as we will see in Chapter 7, their experiences are very mixed indeed. It is also far from clear that access to HE for black people is anything more than an individual solution to a wider social problem of racism. That is, it is doubtful whether wider access can have a broader goal in affecting structures of disadvantage. As will be indicated in the rest of this chapter and in much of the rest of this book, there is a less rosy picture to paint: one in which some groups of black students do badly in access to HE and in which many black students face discrimination once in HE.

There are, therefore, many lacunae in the more optimistic interpretations of the statistical picture. First, black students concentrate in some HEIs, so that many HEIs have very small numbers of such students. This is to do with a set of related factors, including the desire of HEIs to gain more local recruits, the concentration of black people in a few areas of the country and their preference for applying to local HEIs. Modood and Shiner (1994: 5) point to the conclusion in UCCA statistical supplements for 1991 and 1992 that nearly 50 per cent of black applicants applied to the 35 HEIs in the London and South-East regions compared with 20 per cent of white applicants. Second, black applicants tend to apply for courses where competition is high (law, medicine) and hence A level requirements are high (Modood and Shiner, 1994: 5–6). Third, with the exception of Chinese and some groups of Asian students, black students often enter HE after 21 years of age as a result of taking GCSEs after the age of 16 (Jones, 1993: 36–9). Finally – although this list is by no means exhaustive – black students often experience HE as isolating and discriminatory when they get there. The basic point is that the bald statistical picture is open to a range of interpretations, only some of which would reveal a real and marked increase in accessibility; and where accessibility is a far wider notion than simply getting into courses in HE.

The difficulties of operationalizing the idea of under-representation are illustrated if we again take the issue of age and relate this to how past imbalances and underrepresentations might be redressed. Having recognized that black people have a younger age structure than whites, then simple percentage figures for entry to HE would have to recognize the potentially greater numbers of black people seeking entry (Jones, 1993). As suggested above, this younger age structure indicates that, in the future, large numbers of black students may demand access to HE. Essentially, then, if we find that the proportions of different ethnic minority groups entering HE is greater than their representation in the population, our understanding of that would need to recognize age structures. Paradoxically, there could still be exclusion in this situation, with far greater numbers demanding access to HE than are getting it. There is, therefore, no simple relationship between population figures and figures for entry to HE. In other words, the idea of underrepresentation, on which so much hangs, is a contested and political one. Part of the contestation relates to a crude linking of figures on access to HE to census figures, followed by a conclusion that enough has been done, that equity has arrived.

If we recognize that underrepresentation is open to a number of interpretations, then so will be discussions of how we redress these imbalances. If black students have not had equal access to HE for a considerable period of time (we cannot know the history of unequal access statistically as ethnic entry data have only recently been collected) then the interpretation of figures for entry would need to recognize this. There is, of course, a complex policy and political issue here about what would constitute a redressing of imbalances in access. Where black students have experienced exclusion from HE for a considerable time, redressing that may require not only many years of action but also levels of recruitment which, on the face of it, look substantial. As we will see, this can produce fears about falling standards and about the possible exclusion of those students who have accessed HE, with relative ease, in the past. As with many 'fears' in the area of race, these are not real: standards are not falling in order to admit black students, even though they may be falling generally and for other reasons; white students are not being excluded by their inclusion. These fears are, however, real in their consequences.

There is a final point which links with strategies to redress imbalances and, in many ways, highlights many of the arguments that are being developed here: 'Strikingly, the evidence that some groups ... enjoy above average levels of representation [in HE] suggests that the result of any future anti-discrimination measures will be to consolidate the over-representation of some minorities' (Modood, 1993: iv). This view not only avoids a discussion of what representation means but also locates the future of anti-discrimination measures in access issues. The point is surely that even if we recognize that there is differential access for groups of black students, with some groups consistently at the bottom of rank orderings of success, there is still the possibility that their experiences in HE and what happens when they enter the labour market are similar and that a significant element of any anti-discrimination measures should deal with that set of problems.

Positive action

Without discussing further what often seems to be a systematic confusion of positive action and positive discrimination, we must recognize that many people, including academics, appear to be confused. This is indicated in the views on admissions policies and on ethnic monitoring of HE admissions tutors who put forward opinions ranging from 'we practise positive discrimination', to 'we do not undertake positive discrimination', to 'ethnic origin is of absolutely no relevance to admissions' (Bird *et al.*, 1992b).

We can be fairly clear what positive action is. It is about redressing imbalances which are the result of past and/or present discrimination, and has legal backing in the Race Relations Act of 1976 and the Sex Discrimination Act of 1975. In the context of the 1976 Race Relations Act, it is quite clear what employers can legally and legitimately do. They can encourage people from ethnic minorities to take advantage of employment opportunities where they are underrepresented; they can train ethnic minorities for work where they are underrepresented; and they can train people of particular racial groups to meet the special needs of those groups. Encouragement could include using the ethnic minority press for advertising; training could include management development training or funding outside trainers to train potential employees (RREAS, 1991: 2–5). Underrepresentation is a complex issue, but includes reference to the proportion of ethnic minorities in the organization or in the community where the organization exists. Although positive action programmes have primarily been developed in the context of employment, they can also be developed with reference to access to HE. In the case of entry to HE, there could be measures by which suitably qualified people from minority ethnic groups are encouraged to apply for entry. In addition, there might also be measures to give education/ training to improve the chances of success in the admissions game for those who lack the necessary formal qualifications. An example here would be Access courses for mature black students who missed out on post-16 education. In these two contexts, positive action would include equality of access to information, fair and equitable marketing procedures and access to an educational environment which values ethnic differences in, for example, the curriculum. What, then, of the aims of positive action strategies? The aim is simple, and that is to provide fair(er) competition, to make the grounds on which competition for places occurs more equal and to equalize the chances of success once in HE.

The other side of this coin is what positive action is *not*; that is, what would, in effect, constitute positive discrimination. Positive action is not: selecting a student because he or she is black; selecting black students simply to get an ethnic balance in an institution; preferential treatment; action simply to improve an institution's image; the setting of admissions *quotas* with sanctions if these are not met. On this latter point, positive action can include the setting of *targets*, such as targets for recruitment over a given time period. As will be suggested later, targets are a very good way of assessing whether an institution's positive action strategies, as these relate to recruitment, are working.

Having briefly discussed the statistics and how they might relate to positive action strategies, we could review the situation in the following simple sentence. Significant numbers of black people do enter HE and are often successful. As already suggested, few HEIs ethnically monitor progression and outcomes, so there is no clear national picture, although some studies (Singh, 1990; Kibble, n.d.), suggest that experiences in HE may sometimes adversely effect performance. This brings us to two issues central to the whole debate about rhetorics and realities: the barriers which still face many black people seeking entry to HE; and the internal barriers to those who are successful in entering HE. That some succeed does not mean that discrimination is absent, but often means that people succeed despite the discrimination. In the rest of this chapter I would like to indicate the nature of these barriers, so that in subsequent chapters strategies to overcome barriers can be studied.

Barriers to access have been widely discussed in previous literature; however, barriers to progression once in HE have received considerably less attention from researchers. It is significant that both HEIs, in their mission statements, and researchers have focused on access to the near exclusion of progression. What we will do here is take up issues of both access and progression as identified by a representative group of black students interviewed in a number of schools and HEIs in the Bath and Bristol areas. There seems to be every reason to see this group of students as representative of black students elsewhere. They were carefully selected and interviewed by a black person in a supportive setting, with guarantees of confidentiality. They were drawn from both local and national catchment areas, were from a range of social class backgrounds and a range of ethnic groups, and included both men and women. There is also every reason to take their views seriously and at face value as indicative of what hinders progression to, and success in, HE and of the sorts of strategies that could be developed to enhance access and progression. There was also a very strong feeling on the part of the interviewers – and this was often backed up by comments from interviewees – that this was the first time they had been given the opportunity to talk about experiences of school and HE in a relatively neutral setting; that is, one in which staff from school or HE were absent. The veracity of interviews has a lot to do with those facilitating them and the nature of the environment in which they are occurring. The safe setting, coupled with a stringent avoidance of raising issues of racial discrimination as part of the structure of the interview process, makes the views of these students particularly convincing and challenging. Where issues of race and discrimination were discussed, they were raised by the interviewees.

Interlude

It will be useful here to paint brief pictures of the five schools and three HEIs involved in the Bath and Bristol study, as it is the views of their students that form a great deal of what is to follow, both in terms of school and HE experience and in terms of strategies to enhance access and progression.

School A: a selective, inner-city school in a largely middle-class neighbourhood with a very small number of black students, predominantly of Asian origin. The school selects through a verbal reasoning test and there is a high demand for places. The school has regularly sought to give up its selective, grammar school status, but without the support of the Secretary of State for Education. As with all schools in the study, 'School A' has an anti-racist policy. There is a large sixth form with significant numbers of students entering higher education. The staffing in the school is predominantly white.

School B: a comprehensive, all-girls school with a small proportion of black students, mainly of Asian and Chinese origin. The school is in an area where most secondary education is single-sex. The school expects most pupils to do A levels and to enter higher education. The staffing in the school in predominantly white.

School C: an inner-city comprehensive in which about 20 per cent of the students are black, mainly Afro-Caribbean and Chinese. Of all the schools in the study, 'School C' has the most developed anti-racist policy and practice, which has been commended by HMI. The school has a small, but successful, sixth form. As with the other schools, the staffing is predominantly white.

School D: an inner-city, selective school with a very small sixth form and in which between 20 and 30 per cent of the students are black, mainly of Afro-Caribbean origin and from the local community. The issue of its selective status is an acute one, in that it is in competition with school A and, in fact, really does not need selection in order to recruit sufficient students. Post-16 staying on rates are low, with numbers of students either doing GCSE resits in year 12 or going to local further education colleges. This school had been the subject of frequent needs analyses. Hence there was a scepticism about further research: 'the children are bored and tired of being guinea pigs . . . many black parents are sick and tired of their children being singled out for research' (deputy head, unpublished transcript). The school has few black staff but one black teacher is in the senior management team.

School E: another inner-city comprehensive, in which 20 per cent of the students are black, the majority Afro-Caribbean. As with a number of the schools this one has few black staff but a strong commitment to race equality. The school has a small sixth form, which recruits small numbers of black students. However, progression to HE is not particularly common.

City Polytechnic: a large multi-site polytechnic (now a university), with the main site on the outskirts of the city. Despite a mission to serve local communities and a developed system of access courses provided at local further education colleges, the polytechnic recruits relatively small numbers of black students, certainly less than the percentage (5–6 per cent) of black people in the local population. The majority of those black students enter a small number of programmes, in particular social work, teacher education and business studies.

City College of HE: a small college of higher education specializing in teacher education and humanities, and with a developing interest in access course provision and in recruiting more black students from the local area.

City University: a traditional university in the city centre with an international reputation for teaching and research. Although the institution as a whole has no specific policy to widen access to black students, some departments, including social work, see this as part of their mission and have already developed access course links with further education colleges; this department seeks to recruit local black students from access courses. The majority of black students at the university are overseas students and, in some programmes – for example, masters degrees in education – more or less all the students are black overseas students.

Barriers to access

When asked to reflect on barriers, the Bath and Bristol students focused, as one might expect, on experiences of school. Barriers to access included lack of information about HE available both to them and to parents, the quality of careers advice, teacher attitudes towards progression post-16 and the curriculum. Many students – and most often Afro-Caribbean students – knew little about HE, were not encouraged to think about HE by careers teachers and were sometimes discouraged from thinking about post-16 education by other teachers. Many of these students were less likely than their white counterparts to do A level courses in years 12 and 13, and more likely to be resitting GCSEs (see Jones, 1993: 31–60, for national data). They were often of the opinion that the courses they were studying neither met their needs nor made any attempt to include perspectives on what they saw as their cultural heritage.

Barriers are related to at least three variables: race, gender and social class. For example, Afro-Caribbean girls and Asian boys received considerably more support from schools for post-16 study than did Afro-Caribbean boys and Asian girls. For the latter, the assumption seemed to be that they are not up to study in HE or that parents would not support such aspirations. In addition, Asian and African students from privileged backgrounds, in terms of income and wealth, received more support from parents and schools than did Afro-Caribbean and Bangladeshi students from less privileged backgrounds. There was, however, a widespread feeling among the students that issues of race were especially significant in how they were treated at school and hence in the likelihood of progression to HE. Race issues arose, for the students, in more or less overt forms: on the one hand, active discouragement to consider education post-16 despite GCSE success; on the other hand, lack of readily available and quality careers advice. This typical response from Michael, an Afro-Caribbean student, illustrates these points: 'University was not even mentioned, nobody thought I would go there, that was the general attitude of the whole school. I actually remember my careers teacher laughing at me when I said that I was applying to university and she actually told me to forget it . . . it was a 3 minute conversation and got me very angry.'

There were particular problems where black students were a very small minority in school, as in school B. Here they experienced isolation and, in some cases, overt discrimination:

Question: I am sure you will meet another Indian girl.
Answer: It would be nice because I am the only one who is coloured in my year. (Rehana, Asian girl)

Question: Are the teachers OK?
Answer: I had this feeling in history . . . I was the only black girl in the class, which is not unusual, but she [the teacher] kept making me feel really inadequate, she kept saying things like 'Oh, why are you so different from everyone else?' . . . I did tell my mum but I did not want her to get involved . . . I told her not to say anything, it would probably get better but it didn't . . . I just slowly went down hill. (Dawn, Afro-Caribbean girl)

Attitudes to post-16 education and the quality of careers advice were often felt to be about a divide between academic education, which was more likely to be recommended to white, Chinese and some groups of Asian students, and vocational education, which was for other groups of black students. 'It has got a long history where West Indians have not been encouraged to do anything but sport . . . Asians are different . . . they have been encouraged in terms of business and economics [and] there has always been a push to science' (Nibden, an Asian man).

This process is exemplified by a group of Afro-Caribbeans in one school, who were consistently offered CPVE courses rather than GCSE resits or GCE A levels. As Sonja, an Afro-Caribbean girl, put it: 'I talked to X [the careers teacher] . . . and she thought that I would do CPVE . . . I really don't want to do CPVE but the teacher thought it would be better for me . . . I was pressured into taking the CPVE course . . . instead I wanted to take all the GCSEs.' This particular example supports Gillborn's (1990: 138–41) finding that teachers disproportionately enquired about Afro-Caribbean pupils' subject choices but also regularly recommended different choices of lower academic status.

At the back of many of the comments by students there was, therefore, a concern with racially discriminatory attitudes and behaviours. This was put in a variety of ways, all of which are telling.

A lot more black parents need to be aware of what is going on in schools and not trust teachers so much ... A lot of white people in schools are very happy to think that they are not racist, [but] they don't even recognize what we [black students] are talking about.

(Annette, Afro-Caribbean)

For us, it is getting the black perspective [in] and developing and refining that ... feeding that into courses ... because most of the material they are using for white pupils entrenches racism and is racist material.

(Spencer, Afro-Caribbean)

Society doesn't want to see black people in a positive role at all ... a lot of black people know they've got a positive identity, but trying to convince white people ... no, you can't do it.

(Janice, Afro-Caribbean)

This view of the importance of a black perspective in school and the significance of positive role models was frequently discussed in the context of the lack of black teachers. As Gaynor, an Afro-Caribbean girl, put it: 'if there was a black teacher I [could] talk to them ... I reckon there would be racism, behind the teacher's back they'd call them names, goodness knows what they would call a black teacher.'

Finally, we need to refer to teacher views. These are, as might be expected, equivocal. There is, first, some recognition of discrimination:

There is still a hidden institutional racism which children pick up from junior school onwards. Most children were well aware of covert racism although for many teachers the idea is an anathema and is likely to be immediately rejected. There is still a prevalent image amongst teachers that those who seek to eradicate or challenge racism in schools are the least popular.

(Geoff)

Second, there is some recognition of the divisiveness of provision. As Sarah put it, 'although there are few minority ethnic groups in the fifth year [year 11], there is a lot in the school as a whole, especially in lower years.' This is developed by Dave in a rather contradictory statement, 'apart from the CPVE group ... there is no channelling of ethnic minority groups and they certainly wouldn't be treated differently', and by Chris: 'The majority of black kids are in lower bands ... the school states that students are able to change bands, but we have no record of how frequently this occurs ... If a student has been in a low band throughout the school it is too late for them to have high aspirations.' Finally, there is some interest in the background of black children as this relates to schooling, but that interest is a curious mixture of accuracy and stereotyping.

Black girls generally want to settle down and get a steady job. There are many Asian girls who don't want to do anything because they are getting married anyway.

(Steve)

There can be a tremendous parental drive to push children beyond their abilities. This is more true of white middle class and Asian parents . . . who want their sons to be accountants etc. Asian parents are perceived as definitely more interested and pushy in regard to their children's education than Afro-Caribbean parents.

(Margaret)

As we will see later, referring to the ethnic background of black students as an important explanation of why they do not seek access to HE is also common among the HE staff, and often goes hand-in-hand with an unwillingness to include structural factors in such an explanation.

The sum of all these perceptions suggests that the success of many black students in gaining entry to HE is, for many of them, to be set against a background of discouragement in schools, stereotyping and lack of understanding. It is therefore possible that some groups of black students are succeeding in spite of considerable discrimination and discouragement, while others face significantly more encouragement from both teachers and parents. While some of these differences may relate to gender and social class (for example, in the different treatments which Asian boys and girls and Afro-Caribbean boys and girls face), it is unlikely, from the evidence of the Bath and Bristol students, that many had lives in which racial discrimination, in and out of school, was absent. Even where schools had anti-racist policies and practices, black students and some staff took the view that such policies were of limited effect in influencing what happens outside the classroom and in less formal situations.

Internal barriers to progression and quality in higher education

As already suggested, black entry to higher education is, by any standards, a sign of success, but success which should not lead us to ignore barriers within HEIs to those who have entered. Put another way, the public face and rhetoric of HE – accessibility aligned with quality and standards – has largely ignored the implications of greater diversity in the student body. As suggested in the Andrew Dorn quotation above (p. 10), considerable work is required even to get discrimination on to the agenda for discussion in HE; after all, how can liberal institutions discriminate when liberals do not, by self-definition, discriminate? As will become clear below (especially in Chapter 4), there is a variety of views from staff on discrimination in HEIs. There are those who deny its existence and those who see it as a minority thing, which is merely a reflection of the wider society. There is another group which recognizes that discrimination is widespread and reacts to this in two opposed ways: one which borders on self-hatred and paralysis as against one which sees the possibility of at least ameliorating discrimination.

The reality is, if a substantial number of black students in HE are to be believed, one in which discrimination is common, even if not always overt or recognized. It is this very covertness of discrimination that makes it difficult to tackle. We can take three examples of internal barriers in HE which may effect progression and success for black students: the attitudes and behaviours of what are predominantly white staff and students; feelings of isolation and lack of support for black students; the curricula which are on offer to black students.

Staff and student attitudes and behaviours

It was over staff and students' attitudes and behaviour that black students were most vociferous. The following is a sample of views:

> You are getting white people talking and lecturing about racism and yet they won't confront their own racism.
>
> > (Barrington, Afro-Caribbean)

> He [a black student] was looked down upon . . . one of his lecturers said something like 'I don't think I'm going to see you next year, you won't be here' . . . he was waiting to kick him off the course basically.
>
> > (Yvonne, Afro-Caribbean)

> When I have done placements I am very conscious that I am an Asian and [that] is not very common . . . I am aware of racism.
>
> > (Rakesh, Asian)

> Where is this equal opportunity thing?
>
> > (Angela, Afro-Caribbean)

> There was no black tutor to relate to [even though] there is a high percentage of us [black students] here.
>
> > (Interjit, Asian)

> Most students are quite liberal but they will crack jokes but you have got to know when people are joking or being vindictive; there is a fine dividing line.
>
> > (Michael, Afro-Caribbean)

> [We] have a discussion on different topics – racism, stereotyping, stuff like that . . . a lot of [white students] said *we're* being racialist.
>
> > (Phil, Afro-Caribbean)

I don't see any black or Asian lecturers . . . if there was a black or Asian lecturer, how would he be received by all the white students . . . I think the way things are they would not be received well.

(Shaffique, Asian)

The issues here are many and complex: the extent of discrimination by staff and students in schools and HE; the effectiveness or otherwise of positive action to increase black academic recruitment in schools and HE; the impact of the failure to achieve this on the feelings of isolation of black students. What is clear is that discriminatory practices and attitudes are common. These range from the more overt, in which, as in the quotation from Yvonne, attention is drawn to the failings of black students in an open way in front of other students, to the more covert views, implied in Phil's statement, which include an unwillingness to consider that courses and curricula may not effectively address issues of race and discrimination. The covertness of discrimination is particularly problematic. The combination of liberalism and joking experienced by Michael is an interesting example, in that it indicates that people are not once-and-for-all liberal or illiberal, but combine elements of both. However, it also suggests a problem for black students, in that they have to experience that combination and deal with it; that is, it becomes their responsibility to decide whether there is discrimination. In this context the idea of a dividing line is especially appropriate. The behaviour of white students serves to divide and exclude, overtly or covertly, and the black students have to decide not only if lines of division are being drawn but what to do about that process. It remains unclear whether HE policies on racial harassment are effective here. As with many policies in this area, the simple existence of a policy is no guarantee that black students will complain of harassment or that institutions will seek to deal with grievances in an effective manner. In part, the problem is that policies are perceived to be ineffective and to put the responsibility on the potential victim to make a complaint. There is rarely, therefore, a proactive stance on issues of harassment; rather, policy is reactive and complainant driven.

As we will see below, many academic staff in HE are unaware of what discrimination is, of its extent and of what redress there is for those who feel themselves to be discriminated against. In addition, they are uneasy about the relationships between issues of discrimination and the curriculum. In general, this can be put in a more pointed fashion. Comparing student and staff views of ethnic diversity in HE (Bird *et al.*, 1992a, b, c), there seems to be more awareness of the issues, and more reflexivity, on the part of black students than on that of the majority of white staff and students. This is not to claim that the victims of discrimination have the greatest understanding, but involves a claim that they have something important to say and that white staff and students – lacking significant contact with black staff and students – may often lack understanding and empathy. Empathy and understanding are, in this context, complex and difficult ideas. They may neither be what black people want nor indicate an adequate response to long-standing structures of discrimination. However, the lack of them within structures which are unfamiliar and alien is likely to be especially isolating.

The isolation of black students

> I did not like the Department much ... I found it very frustrating being the only Asian; for example, you would get the feeling that you were the token minority.
>
> (Hemlata, Asian)

> I did not get enough support from the tutors on the course because ... I don't think they were able to relate to black students.
>
> (Marcus, Afro-Caribbean)

> I just felt very visible and the first thing I noticed I was the only black face in the group ... I was not getting abuse or anything, I just felt uncomfortable.
>
> (Jittinder, Asian)

> It was fairly inhibiting to carry the flag [against] racism.
>
> (Barrington, Afro-Caribbean)

> There should be a black person who they can go to see with problems. They have an overseas one, but not one for blacks born here ... [and] at interviews for HE there were no Asian and ethnic minority [staff].
>
> (Wasim, Asian)

There are, in these views, two contexts of isolation: that felt by black students who are in a substantial minority in HEIs which primarily recruit white students and that experienced by very many black students when faced with academic and administrative staff who are rarely black. The first context suggests that where there are many black students, as there often are in departments training social workers and teachers, some support is gained by the very presence of other black students. The second, however, indicates that even where support from other students is available, the lack of black staff is still a central issue. While the presence of black staff may well not be a sufficient condition for dealing with isolation of students, it is probably a necessary one. We therefore would contest Ross's (1990) view that the necessity for black staff in HE if black students are to succeed is a comfortable but none the less mistaken myth. In particular, such staff can act as role models for black students. Their position *vis-à-vis* white students is more equivocal. A liberalism in white students cannot be assumed any more than can the liberalism of HEI staff. To take one example from the Bath and Bristol study, in one HEI an Asian member of staff faced considerable problems from white students (unpublished transcript). In particular, white women students said that his behaviour was overpowering and patriarchal and that this was how Asian men behave to women. The issue was not successfully resolved and the extent to which the views of the white students were stereotypical and were influencing how they interpreted his behaviour was left undiscussed. As will be suggested below, attempts to deal with discrimination by white staff will be less effective if nothing is done to address the attitudes and behaviours of white students.

Isolation is felt in a multiple sense: isolation from peers where there are few black people on a course; isolation from white students, some of whom actively discriminate; isolation within largely white institutions; isolation from parents and parental cultures. Greater degrees of isolation are expressed by Asian students in general, and by Asian women students in particular. Significantly, these students feel isolation even though they have often had strong teacher and parental encouragement to enter HE and are successful in gaining entry.

The curriculum

On the face of it the curriculum might not be seen as a problem for black students in HE. As one HE tutor put it, 'Most of my colleagues here would say no [to a multicultural approach]' (Bird *et al.*, 1992b: 24). This contrasts nicely with what some black students said:

> For us [the important] thing is getting the black perspective and . . . feeding that into courses.
>
> > (Phil, Afro-Caribbean)

> First of all, you'd have to start teaching black history instead of teaching English history . . . [that is] teaching history so people have respect for people . . . My frustration comes from two cultures so that I see things from a different perspective . . . they did not take much interest in ethnic or oriental theatre.
>
> > (Shayla, Asian)

Tutors, particularly those in science and engineering, were very defensive about the curriculum, seeing it as, in various ways, sacrosanct and free from social influences. This is best summed up in the views of three members of staff teaching courses in science and engineering subjects: 'Chem. eng. is chem. eng. no matter what the skin colour.' 'I am not sure what a multicultural approach would mean in the context of science.' 'Engineering *is* engineering' (Bird *et al.*, 1992b: 24).

Students, on the other hand, regularly draw attention to gaps in the curriculum – no recognition that algebra was an Arab invention, no recognition of black historians and so on. As with experiences of isolation, Asian students more often drew attention to lack of cultural awareness within HE curricula than did other groups of black students. While there is some meeting of minds – multicultural inputs into history, social sciences, social work training – the meeting is usually with *individual* tutors on a *limited* range of courses. Multiculturalism is rarely part of the policy agenda in HE, nor is the curriculum seen as a site for non-curricular interference. From staff comes a somewhat narrow idea of the curriculum, which is seen as primarily course content and knowledge. Wider curriculum issues – assessment of courses, their delivery, the wider institutional environment and ethos – are seen as technical and managerial issues rather than political ones. This is the danger of liberalism which Gilroy, citing Hall, draws attention to: 'the "race" issue has been seen from the vantage point of sympathetic liberalism as a matter of policy rather than politics' (Gilroy, 1987: 150). The implication of this view is that race issues are not to do with structures of power and, once recognized, any problems around race will be resolved by technical changes which will occur without difficulty and resistance. These technical solutions are often the very same things that are believed, in HE, to make the system more generally flexible and responsive; that is, modularization, Credit Accumulation and Transfer Schemes (CATS), Accreditation of Prior Experiential Learning (APEL) and suchlike.

While multi-culturalism in the curriculum is part of what Charles Taylor calls a politics of recognition (Taylor and Gutmann, 1992), there are, beyond the nuts and bolts of how to make curricula more responsive to diversity of clients, two difficult issues for HE: first, whether multi-culturalism works; second, whether it ignores, as has been argued in the context of its use in schools, issues of racism (Stone, 1980). In addressing the first issue we can say that knowledge of other cultures is of limited significance if it is not accompanied by greater understanding of how some cultures are devalued and discriminated against. If we ask the question, 'Does knowledge of other cultures yield tolerance?', then there is a less than clear verdict on this. The idea of tolerance is, itself, problematic. As Mendus (1989) suggests, tolerance can often have a patronizing and discriminatory meaning, associated, for example, with how we 'put up with' naughty children. Hage (1994) takes the issue further and argues that tolerance is, in Bourdieu's terms, a strategy of condescension which is used by powerful people in their dealing with the less powerful. Hage cites a particularly illuminating example in discussing political reactions in Australia to the harassment of Arab Australians during the Gulf War:

> Instead of saying: 'there are some Australian citizens who are capable of terrorising other Australian citizens and getting away with it. We must not allow them to have this power', the Prime Minister ends up implying that: 'there are some Australian citizens who are capable of terrorising other Australian citizens and getting away with it. Be charitable and support the victims'. Not only does this kind of statement leave the power of the racist unchallenged. It does not even empower the victims of racism to resist. It reduces them to helpless people one is encouraged to protect and be charitable to.
>
> (Hage, 1994: 25)

In addition, the idea that knowledge leads to understanding involves a commitment to an Enlightenment view that knowledge is the road to ridding individuals and social groups of intolerance and hatred. Some reservations over this view are suggested in some unpublished work in schools in Bristol (Simmons-Bird, 1992), which suggests that racist name calling increased significantly following attempts to make history and geography more multicultural; that is, to increase information flows going to white students and to educate them out of stereotypical views of black people. What seems clear is that even if knowledge of others and understanding of them are not automatically linked, *lack* of understanding of others, and exclusion of them from access to a responsive curriculum, results in a lack of recognition and is, in that sense, discriminatory. As to a second issue – the relationships between teaching about multi-cultural issues and, as a result, missing structural issues of discrimination and racism – there is no clear picture from the HE point of view. What is clear is that curriculum development in HE often does focus on cultural issues rather than structural ones. Where structural issues arise they tend to do so in dedicated modules on race and ethnicity rather than across the whole curriculum. With reference to both race and gender, such issues need to be integrated into the whole programme. To provide dedicated courses may marginalize race and gender issues and provide a rationale for not dealing with them elsewhere.

In summary, we can say that much of the material relating to barriers to entry to HE and internal barriers facing those who enter relate to issues of discrimination. These issues include a complex of factors: discriminatory attitudes and practice; attitudes and practices which range from the overtly to the covertly discriminatory, from the derisory to the charitable. We can distinguish, therefore, between those attitudes and behaviour which are relatively uncommon in that they involve overt and direct discrimination, and those which are more common but serve to discriminate in a more covert and indirect manner.

Direct and indirect discrimination

If it is correct that, as Dorn (1991) indicates, issues of discrimination are often not on the agenda in HE, there is, in fact, a legal framework and guidelines for its application available to both HEIs and students. The frameworks and guidelines provide definitions of direct and indirect discrimination as well as indications as to how such ideas can be translated into practice. Direct discrimination – which is, in fact, rare and was declared illegal under the Race Relations Act of 1976 – could involve HEIs developing entry criteria which overtly exclude black applicants, or simply saying that black applicants need not apply. However, the idea of indirect discrimination indicates how easily discrimination can become covert, and can be either intended or unintended: 'Indirect racial discrimination consists of treatment which may be described as equal in a formal sense as between different racial groups but is discriminatory in its effects on one particular racial group' (CRE, 1989a).

In the context of what has been said above concerning black students' access to HE and the barriers operating for those who are successful, we can argue that there is a number of potential, and often actual, practices which could operate in an indirectly discriminatory fashion. Two examples can illustrate the point. First is the use of assessment criteria which assume that students are uniform in cultural, linguistic, religious and other lifestyle experiences. There is therefore the possibility that the use of group work and group assessment may indirectly discriminate if some groups, for cultural reasons, find group work difficult or threatening. This is an argument that also has implications for gender discrimination, particularly if men students monopolize teacher/tutor time and dominate the organization of work. Second is the selection of students using criteria which exclude more of a certain ethnic group than could be justified educationally, perhaps, by a reliance on A levels and A level points, or the ignoring of other, more vocational qualifications. As suggested above (pp. 11–12), Afro-Caribbean students are more likely to take vocational qualifications than either white or other minority ethnic groups. The potentially discriminatory effects of relying on A levels are recognized but not much researched. As Modood and Shiner (1994: 47) put it,

> It could be argued that our very definition of 'academic performance' . . . may itself be indirectly discriminatory against some ethnic groups. It assumes that A level scores and resits are valid criteria for academic selection. If, however, these criteria are not valid (if there is no special relation between them and final degree results) and yet they disproportionately disadvantage certain ethnic minority groups, then there could be a case that they are discriminatory.

There is a double issue here. While many staff in HE recognize that A levels have limited relevance to study, they recognize that they can operate as an effective rationing device for student places. As one HE tutor put it, 'Frankly, I find it extremely difficult to judge potential other than by examination results . . . and certainly to judge potential in a realistic amount of time with the number applicants we get' (Bird *et al.*, 1992b, unpublished transcript). This view about convenience is not accompanied by any awareness that such rationing may disadvantage black students more than others. As Modood and Shiner suggest, such a possibility seems to be on no one's research agenda. If it were, and if GCE A level scores *were* identified as indirectly discriminatory, this would have profound effects on how HEIs select students and might, for example, lead them to think out more clearly what potential for HE means and therefore be more explicit in identifying and publishing entry criteria.

This potential for indirect discrimination against black students is, of course, set by the system itself. Even though governments recommend that higher education be available to all who have the potential to benefit, there are clearly problems with how we assess that potential and how we ration places among the potentially very large numbers with such potential. It is precisely around these two issues that discrimination can occur. Rationing of places may occur through more than the reliance on particular types of qualification and over what time period they were gained, such that students are believed to need three A levels taken over no more than two sittings. The use of student references, an unwillingness to be clear about what a potential HE student is like and an avoidance of clearly specified entry criteria are all potentially exclusionary (CRE, 1989b: sections 36 and 37, pp. 16–17).[1] All of these might disproportionately and adversely affect black people. In the case of a reliance on GCE A level scores it is unclear whether this is done simply for administrative convenience or whether staff think that GCE A levels tell us something about degree performance. The difficulty is that what is seen as administrative convenience may spill over into indirectly discriminatory action almost without this being recognized as happening.

The lessons here are, however, simple and stark: HEIs have a duty not to discriminate, but many staff in HE do not know and understand the legal framework and the potential for indirect discrimination (Bird *et al.*, 1992c).

Black access to HE in context

As indicated in the introduction, there is a small but growing body of literature on the black experience of access to HE. A minor part of this work deals with progression within HE. As suggested, some of the conclusions of this work are positive, including the high proportions – when compared with white students – of black students who stay in school or college post-16 and enter HE post-18. Equally clearly, there is, as Singh (1990), for example, argues, a paucity of information about which courses and institutions black students enter, how well they do in them and what happens to them on completion. Singh's general conclusions can be taken as representative of much of the work on black students and higher education and include: (a) their concentration in the former polytechnics and colleges of higher education; (b) problems in progression for some groups of black students, such as Afro-Caribbean men, and for black students on some professional courses, such as law (see Kibble, n.d.); and (c) limited payoffs from higher education in terms of later employment. The differentials in progression rates for some groups of black students when compared with white occurs against a background in which any significant gap between them in educational performance is declining (Jones, 1993: 41–3). As we are arguing, some of this differential relates to experiences which black students have of HE, experiences which include discrimination and isolation.

Finally, it is worth noting that many of the authors who are contributing to this developing picture of black students in HE recognize that the statistical picture is, at national, local and institutional levels, inadequate and that there have been few attempts to ask black students about their experiences of compulsory and post-compulsory education. As will be argued in Chapters 6 and 7, there is a need for more adequate and comprehensive ethnic monitoring at institutional level and a need for the funding councils to take such monitoring seriously; for example, in relating teaching quality assessment to institutional missions, especially where these emphasize the recruitment of black students.

Conclusions

Despite the undoubted success which some HEIs have had in recruiting black students and the powerful rhetorics of access which these institutions espouse, there are still considerable barriers to access to, and progression through, such institutions facing these students. The intention behind what follows is to look at some strategies to overcome barriers to both access and progression. The two – access and progression – must be taken together. If we are only interested in access (that is, in opening up the doors of HE), then we are selling a false prospectus to black students; one which does not draw attention to the internal barriers discussed above. This false prospectus may also lead HEIs to act in ways that are indirectly discriminatory and that, in essence, may infringe those aspects of the law which deal with race discrimination.

What follows in Chapters 2 to 6 is an analysis of a number of strategies to foster access to HE and to provide a quality experience in HE for black students. These strategies were developed through close work with a number of HEIs and schools; although they are, in that sense, particular to those institutions, there is every reason to see them as being of more general and national relevance.

Note

1 Referring directly to further and higher education, the CRE guidelines are very specific. With reference to qualifications, and related to sections 1(1)(b) and 17 of the Act:

> 36. Requiring academic attainment that is in excess of the particular knowledge and skills needed to undertake the course would be indirectly discriminatory if this had the effect of excluding a considerably higher proportion of students from a particular racial group and these requirements could not be shown to be justifiable on educational grounds.
>
> (CRE, 1989b: 17)

With reference to subjective criteria (sections 1(1)(b) and 17 of the Act):

> The application of non-academic criteria in determining admissions, particularly where courses are over-subscribed and there is a supply of well-qualified

candidates, may have the effect of excluding disproportionately high numbers of candidates from particular racial groups who are otherwise academically suitable. Where they do so, they would constitute unlawful indirect discrimination if they could not be shown to be justified. Examples of such criteria might include: hobbies; cultural interests; attitudes; sporting activities; family connections; type of school attended; communication skills; and appearance.

(CRE, 1989b: 17)

Part 1

Strategies for Black Access

One perspective on the statistics for recruitment of black students to HE suggests that the reality and the rhetoric of access are close together; the numbers of black people in HE are generally greater than their numbers in the population would suggest (see Chapter 1). In these terms, the missions of many universities to widen access have been achieved. On the other hand, we can take a less optimistic view, both with reference to access and with reference to experience within universities: black students are not spread evenly across HEIs or across courses in HE; they enter HE having experienced discrimination in schools and colleges and expecting to continue to experience it; discrimination *does* continue; the redressing of past imbalances may require even greater recruitment in the future; ethnic monitoring of students in HE is often haphazard and incomplete, such that the regular analysis of their experiences is uncommon.

This part deals with two strategies for widening access to HE for black students, including access into and out of 16–19 education. The first involves HEIs working more closely with schools and the second dissemination of information to black people about what HE has to offer. It is clear that, as was indicated above, despite the success of black students in gaining access to HE, many do so against a background of discouragement and lack of accurate information. In effect, the need for positive action here is twofold: to encourage black students who are suitably qualified to apply to universities and colleges of HE, and to encourage those black students who do not aspire to HE and may not gain qualifications to do so. It is in both these instances that links between schools and HE and the dissemination of quality information can, as will be argued below, be effective.

2

Working with Schools

With W. C. Yee

Many of the initiatives taken to increase numbers of black students in HE have focused on mature students: in other words, students who, for whatever reason, did not complete compulsory education with the necessary qualifications for entry to HE. The targeting of mature black students, particularly through access courses, has been relatively successful. This success might be summed up in the phrase 'education for transformation' (Moodley, 1995), a transformation that may occur either in access courses which are designed exclusively for black students or in ones in which black and white students are included. However, such provision is compensatory; it makes up for what was done badly at an earlier stage. As such, it is an indictment of education up to the age of 16. Working with *schools* may provide an alternative strategy which can, in the future, limit the need for such compensatory provision for mature students. While linking schools and HEIs can form *part* of a strategy to widen access, a more comprehensive strategy would also have to include work within schools – for example, to tackle racial harassment – and within HEIs – for example, to develop responsive curricula and modes of delivery of courses.

Work with five inner-city schools with proportions of black students ranging from 5 to 30 per cent in the Bath and Bristol areas, where there are four HEIs, produced a depressing picture common to many urban areas nationally. Few of the black students had ever visited the HEIs; few had been told about the HEIs and about what they had to offer; few aspired to HE; many saw HEI as not for them, but for bright, middle-class and white students. As Michael, the Afro-Caribbean student already quoted above, said, 'University was not even mentioned, nobody thought I would go there, that was the attitude of the whole school.'

Existing strategies for linking HEIs and schools are very diverse, ranging from the traditional system of schools liaison, with occasional visits by HEI admissions personnel to schools from whom HEIs traditionally recruit, to formal links between one or more HEIs and a number of schools in the locality, region or more widely. Because much traditional liaison only links with schools which already have an HE culture, these systems are likely to be of limited effectiveness in widening access for black students. This is one of the lessons from Mortimore's study, which reveals that black students tend to be concentrated in the least effective schools (cited in Troyna and Carrington, 1990). The systems of liaison developed by HEIs typically involve their staff visiting schools, colleges, conventions, admissions conferences and suchlike, often both nationally and internationally. Few personnel in HE visit local schools; fewer visit inner-city schools. In addition, staff and students in many inner-city schools rarely visit HEIs. This rather traditional system also includes very little coordinated work between the HEIs; in essence, they frequently work with schools as competitors for students, even where such competition might place a burden on schools faced with independent approaches from a number of different institutions. As one teacher put it in the Bath and Bristol study, 'HEIs don't know what each other are doing, even in the same locality ... even faculties in the same institution work independently [with schools]' (unpublished transcript).

The important point is that there is much dissatisfaction with the more traditional ways that HEIs relate to schools. Part of that is based on the quite reasonable belief that a lack of coordination in such work will only serve to overburden school staff further. Another part is to do with the perceived lack of effectiveness of such relationships, especially in involving schools without an HE culture. Finally, teachers in Bath and Bristol seemed to be less and less willing to be involved in such traditional activities as year 12 and 13 conferences, HE conventions and suchlike. This was to do with issues of time and resourcing, but also a healthy scepticism about the effectiveness of such activities and the interest which students took in them.

The intention should, therefore, be to develop more effective systems for linking schools and HEIs, and systems which can, in particular, benefit black students. Ineffective systems of liaison with schools involve providing information on HE which is inadequate and inaccessible, excludes schools that lack an HE ethos and is given too late in a student's school career. Effective systems avoid these pitfalls and, as far as black students are concerned, will include some element of role modelling by black HE students and/or successful black professionals. The development of an effective system was one of the aims of the Bath and Bristol initiative.

Developing HE–school links

School C, with a significant number of black students, some 20 per cent, was approached with a view to trialling and developing a link which would go beyond traditional systems of liaison and build on some of the initiatives developed, for example, through the national Community Service Volunteers/British Petroleum (CSV/BP) student tutoring scheme. Discussions with management were long and thorough, and were rooted in a number of worries and concerns on the part of school managers and teachers.

In particular, there was suspicion of the motives of HEIs and why they had suddenly become interested in black students and their progression. Related initiatives had been discussed in the past and had not come to fruition, and school staff felt that the school had, in the past, been a goldfish bowl for researchers. Indeed, the school had had approaches from some of the HEIs involved in this project, but was also seen as an example of good practice in issues of diversity, hence attracting regional and national interest. Second, there was concern over the effects of such links on the school itself. These included worries over the burden of extra work that links with HE could bring and the effects of such work on existing policies and practices as these related to equality issues.

What developed out of long, and often heated, discussions were the parameters for such work. The result was, therefore, a series of agreed principles which would guide school–HE links. First, it was important that such work should link with other things the school was doing; for example, careers advice/guidance. This was particularly important in that the school, like all others, was fully burdened with delivering the required curriculum and responding to rapid and regular changes in educational policy. Second, links should be useful to the school and provide some kind of payoff in both the short and long term. This follows from the competitive environment in which schools increasingly work and the consequent recognition that there must be more than altruistic motives for working with HE. Third, work with HEIs should raise the profile of HE in general and not act as a recruiting device for particular universities. Independent and competitive strategies by HEIs who seek to chase school students seemed to be especially unpopular in the school. Fourth, black students in HE should be involved in the work with school and should have their work either recognized or, if possible, accredited. Such accreditation would go some way to minimizing the extra burden on black students and, in so doing, enhance their performance in HE rather than adversely affecting it. Finally, both black and white school pupils should be involved. The school took a very strong line over this last point, and staff were concerned that black pupils should not be singled out for attention as this might adversely effect other aspects of their anti-racist activities, which emphasized the inclusion of black students in all school activities.

The decision was taken to focus the work on activities involving groups of school students from years 9 to 12 and groups of HE students; or, put another way, to involve HE staff as little as possible. In part, this decision was based on lessons learned from elsewhere. In particular, the student tutoring schemes developed by CSV and BP suggested that school pupils would learn most from contact with students already in HE. It was important to work with school pupils prior to post-16 education, for by then decisions on progression have already been taken. What was not involved at this stage was the development of more formal links with the school (for example, to guarantee places for numbers of students – what are now termed HE Compacts); nor was there any attempt to work with the issue of flexible, non-GCE A level, entry to HE. The primary emphasis, therefore, was on raising the profile of HE and on the dissemination of information about higher education. Although this profile raising and dissemination would benefit *all* students, the heavy involvement of black HEI students was intended to focus much of the benefit on black school students. Indirectly, parents were involved because their approval was sought for the involvement of their children in the activities. This approval was a formal requirement set out by the school and would, it was hoped, begin to place HE on the parental agenda. There was one especially indicative instance of the sensitivity of working with race issues in schools. One parent of a white student complained that white students were being disadvantaged by the initiative and that they were excluded from the work. This was a misperception – both black and white school students were involved – but none the less this parent was fundamentally opposed to this work.

The school and university students developed two sets of activities. The first was based in the schools and aimed at students in years 9 and 10; that is, those students who were considering GCSE choices and beginning to think about career options. The second was based in HE and involved school students from years 11 and 12, most of whom had little knowledge of HE and few of whom were considering entering HE even though they were, for example, often doing GCE A levels.

Activities in school

The fundamental idea behind the activities was to make them as participative and as student-led as possible. In addition, they were to focus on issues that were important for the school pupils, including more information about HE and about how subject choices made in schools influence both HE entry and future careers. The sessions were facilitated by students from a number of HE faculties and from student unions.

The following structure for sessions was developed.

1.   A warm-up, which included a brainstorm on what HE is, what it has to offer. Pupils were asked to say what sort of people go to HE and why they go, and answers were written on flip charts for future use and discussion.

The end product of this warm-up was a view of HE that indicated exclusivity, in particular with reference to social class and to ethnicity; the typical HE student was believed to be white, middle class and not from inner-city Bristol or Bath. The HE students were, of course, able to counter this stereotype both by their very presence as black students and by making data on who goes to HE available. This challenging of stereotypes also formed part of the second aspect of the activities.

2.   The presentation of an HE video, in this case made by the students union, with the opportunity for a question and answer session after. Groups of pupils were each asked to write down two questions arising from the video and these were, as far as possible, answered.

As might be expected, the focus of questioning included issues to do with what courses are available, what someone in school has to do to enter HE and the costs of HE. In addition, black students were concerned about whether they would fit into HE and whether they would be taught, as they were in school, predominantly by white staff.

3.   Exercises related to decision-making about future study, career and work. Students worked in groups of three to five, with a number of exemplary case studies of types of school pupils.

This is a typical example: 'B is having problems deciding about her future. She is the eldest of four children in her family. Her parents work hard running their own small business, so in the evening, after school, she helps out by either working in the business or looking after the younger children. She has to decide soon about her future. Her parents think that although she is a good student and enjoys school, she is needed at home. They also think she will probably get married in the next few years. Given this, they would like her to leave school and help the family until such time as she marries. B either wants to stay on and get more qualifications and then go to college like her cousin did, or else to get a job which will give her some skills – perhaps in a bank. She is doing well with the Compact employer and it is likely that, if she keeps up her good work, there may be a job available. Her teachers say that they are sure she will succeed if she stays on at school or if she gets a job. *What should she do?*'

Each group was asked to choose from a set of options – stay at school for GCE A levels; leave school and get a job; look at other courses at college; take GCE A levels at college; seek careers advice; take a job that offers vocational training – and to say which course of action was the best. All the cases were designed to refer not only to issues of race and ethnicity, but also to issues of class and gender; thus, in the case of B, white girls and black girls could see their situations mirrored in the example. This was important in order to engage the pupils with the activity and because the groups contained both black and white pupils.

Pupils were then asked if there was a consensus over the decisions taken, and asked to say what the crucial factors in decision-making were: for example, parents, school, friends, siblings, their own wants. It was clear that, as far as decision-making was concerned, decisions to leave school or to continue study were being influenced not only by teachers and by the often inadequate advice being given, but also by friends and parents. The multiplicity of factors bearing on career choice – and the school students expressed the view that they were the ones who were *really* taking the decision in the end – emphasized the need for clear, concise, up-to-date and impartial information and guidance.

4.   The final stage was to introduce the issue of race more explicitly by asking two sets of questions: if the ethnicity in the exemplary cases were changed – say from B being seen as white working class to Asian – would the decision be the same? If decisions do change in such circumstances,

then why is this and what can be done if the effects are negative? This was then expanded to relate to the school itself. If student B is Afro-Caribbean, is she more likely to be encouraged to leave school at 16 than if she is Asian?

The views of schools students were consistent with those of many of the HE students quoted elsewhere is this book. That is, they were aware that issues of race could and did affect judgements by schools and HEIs over the potential of students. Therefore, they recognized that issues of ethnicity, as well as ones related to gender and social class, can influence judgements about suitability even when students have nearly identical qualifications and experience.

This structure of sessions was designed to be flexible. Sections can be delivered at different times and over longer or shorter periods of time to suit the schools and students involved. Indeed, there are advantages to a more flexible mode of delivery, including having an HE presence in school over a more extensive period.

For most of the pupils the evaluations of the sessions were very positive, in particular the view that they could learn more about HE in a half day than they knew before and their keenness to visit HE and see it from the customers', i.e. the students', side. There was, in fact, very little resistance to the sessions in school. Although part of this was to do with the novelty of working with HE students, there was also considerable curiosity about what HE students and HE institutions are like. For the school there was direct feedback into careers advice and, in some particular courses, such as sociology, there was useful material for the race, ethnicity, gender and education sections of syllabuses. One area that was particularly stressed was that more information and understanding for pupils would not directly address misconceptions and information deficits on the part of parents; hence the concern to develop information packs for parents (see in this chapter 'Towards more effective partnerships' and Chapter 3).

Activities in higher education

The important point of work within HE was to get pupils – in this case, in years 11 and 12 – into HEIs to see what happens there. It was recognized that, for many pupils, years 11 and 12 were too late as far as aspirations to HE are concerned. It was hoped that once year 11 and 12 students had been to an HE faculty, they would act as communicators of the message that HE can be on the agendas of other students lower down the school. Again, the focus was on using HE students as facilitators, allowing pupils to shadow them through a day in HE: going to classes, using the library, having food and so on. As with the school-based activities, some of the HE students were black, acting, in effect, as role models for school pupils.

Small groups of students were asked which faculties or departments they would like to visit, the choice being related to future HE or careers aspirations. They were offered the opportunity for one-day visits to HE, with HE students acting as hosts. As far as possible, the pupils were given full exposure to what HE has to offer: the more formal system of lectures and seminars, and the less formal systems of entertainment, societies and suchlike. Without being patronized, pupils were exposed to aspects of HE programmes that would not be intimidating.

The point was to make the exposure to HE demanding but also engaging, and in so doing to reveal, as far as possible, the reality of HE. In general, school students attended first-year degree lectures, seminars and practicals. For black students, part of this exposure was similar to that for white students: it included some of the negative side of HE, including large classes, overcrowded facilities and inadequate libraries. Other facets of the exposure affected black school students in particular: this included the near total lack of black lecturers and tutors and the generally small numbers of black students. This exposure to what is close to the reality of HE turned the visits into something completely different from what can happen; that is, they avoided becoming a combination of public relations and marketing. If the end result is to recruit black students then this should only be accomplished by making it clear what black students will face in HE, and this will include many negative factors. Raising expectations beyond what HE can offer – which is often the effect of public relations activities – is only likely to produce subsequent disaffection among students.

The success of the visits can be judged by the demand for more of them, a demand which was not always easy to meet. There was a major problem here in that school pupils' expectations had been raised, sometimes beyond the ability of schools and HEIs to meet them. In particular, schools – in the context of the National Curriculum – could only release students to visit HEIs on a very limited scale. For HEIs, particularly at faculty and departmental levels, there was sometimes the view that, if such initiatives did not directly lead to recruitment, then the necessary time and funding for these would need to be limited. It is important to stress, within HE faculties, that activities to raise aspirations are long term and are unlikely to lead to any recruitment in the short term. These concerns, of course, raise the issue of the aims of school–HE links: the aim of this strategy was to raise aspirations for HE, sug-gesting the potential usefulness of consortia of HEIs working with a range of schools in a planned and coherent fashion. Such consortia will, of course, never fully resolve the contradiction between the desire to serve communities and widen access and the desire for a competitive advantage. In other words, whatever the public rhetorics and agendas, there are always less public ones which can make inter-institutional cooperation difficult to sustain.

Towards more effective partnerships

There are no obvious disadvantages in collaborating, provided that the people involved trust each other and are wholly professional in their conduct.

(School manager contemplating a partnership with HE in
Bird and Yee, 1994: 16)

A wide range of school–HE links are now being developed which go beyond both the traditional model discussed earlier and the links established in Bath and Bristol (Bird and Yee, 1994). Although these are not exclusively designed to access black students, they can provide the basis for such a process. These links now include using students as tutors in schools and the development of formal HE Compacts. There now seems to be a generally agreed set of rules of the game which school–HE partnerships usually follow, and these include the following.

Give students a central role in the link

> It's about positive role modelling. It's about [black] students in schools having people to talk to, people who they can identify with.
> (Black HE student in Bird and Yee, 1994: 16)

> The whole philosophy of the scheme is that students . . . act as suitable, effective mentors to the students who might not go on to higher education . . . one of the reasons they might not is because they don't have the support, don't know what HE is.
> (Staff interviewee in Bird and Yee, 1994: 22)

The essential point is that the HE students will act as role models and the school pupils are, in consequence, more likely to listen to them and learn from them. Where the aim is to work with black students there should be matching of black students in HE with those in school. The CSV/BP system of student tutoring does not seek to match students either in terms of race and gender or in terms of subjects being studied. Matching by ethnicity can, however, be successful to the extent that it is made available should students request it. It is important not to make matching compulsory, if for no other reason than that some students might not want it or need it.

Work across the age range in schools

> We go right through from the infants to the sixth form . . . we've got one [special] school that started this because the students at [FE College X] asked to go to a special school.
> (Staff interviewee in Bird and Yee, 1994: 18)

Effective links with schools will have to recognize that aspirations for HE, including for black students, are being developed at least from the start of secondary school and possibly earlier. Thus, working, as many formal HE Compacts now do, with years 12 and 13 can do little, if anything, to deal with the development of aspirations which occurs in earlier years. The CSV/BP scheme does, therefore, include links with primary schools as well as secondary, in which student tutors work to assist teachers in the classroom with reading, project work and so on. The average load on students is 15 two-hour sessions in a year. Students are, in this scheme, volunteers and receive no recognition or accreditation of their work, and the voluntary nature of this and other schemes does not seem to be a problem for students: 'I think it's a burden that [we're] quite pleased to take on ... By being involved in the scheme it's a way of saying "well, look, I'm trying to do something for you"' (black interviewee, Bird and Yee, 1994: 16). It is probably only issues of resourcing and the availability of students that prevents a greater extension of this variety of work with schools, including more work with primary schools.

Try to develop flexible entry to HE

> We're not saying 'get rid of A level courses' ... what we're really asking ourselves is to look at what criteria we're looking for in a student ... if [we] need three C's that's fine, but we need to be able to justify why we're looking for 3 C's, not just because it's blocking out 1500 applicants.
>
> (Bird and Yee, 1994: 24)

Although there still appears to be a widespread reliance on GCE A levels for entry to HE, flexible entry, including support for GNVQs and advanced GNVQs, working with records of achievement and the development of more general HE entry certificates, is increasingly on the agenda. There is an old argument here concerning the relevance on A levels and their predictive value for success in HE. There is also a more contemporary one about whether the reliance on A levels, often taken at one sitting, indirectly discriminates against black students (Modood and Shiner, 1994: 47–8). There is little evidence that systems of flexible entry which work either with lower GCE A level points or with qualifications other than GCE A levels are seen by students as the equivalent of easier entry (Bird and Yee, 1994). Very often, students who are asked to gain lower GCE A levels points are doing something in addition to GCE A levels, such as a record of achievement; those working with alternatives, including GNVQs, do not see these are easier. We need to recognize that there is a diversity of entry routes to HE and that those routes are of equal value. This will require work with gatekeepers to develop a recognition that different qualifications be judged on equal terms with GCE A levels. In addition, there is a need for some effective way of operationalizing the idea of a potential to benefit from higher education, which can then be related much more explicitly than at present to qualifications.

In the context of black access to HE, recognition of more vocational qualifications might, as argued above, assist some groups; for example, Afro-Caribbean boys. Relating flexible entry to black access is, however, likely to prove a highly political issue, in that it will be easy to argue that a special case is being made for such students which includes 'easier' entry. That such entry routes are not easier may be obvious, but there is a job to be done in decoupling ideas about flexible entry from notions of easier entry, and flexible entry which helps black students from easier entry for them. In this sense, flexible entry which assists black students is best defined as a positive action measure and not, in any sense, as a form of positive discrimination. In other words, only the latter would involve ideas of easy entry or entry where 'normal' standards are not met.

Work with ethnically mixed groups of students

> Singling out black students for attention can be dangerous and divisive ... we are against it *per se.*
>
> (School teacher, unpublished transcript)

Many of the schools involved in links with HE take the view that, although the aim is to target black students and enhance their progression opportunities, work with students should involve ethnically mixed groups. There are two main rationales for this: the fear that singling out black students and working exclusively with them would stigmatize such students and could adversely affect attempts to develop multi-cultural and multi-racial policies and practices; and the hope that mixing black and white students will not only enhance opportunities but also improve relationships between these groups. For the project work discussed above, it was a condition set by the schools that there was work with mixed groups and not with groups of black students on their own. Partly as a result of the positive race policies of the schools involved, mixed groups of students did work well together and there was little tension between black and white students.

As we will see in Chapter 7, there is a deeper reason for the uneasiness about working with ethnically exclusive groups of students, which relates to general attitudes towards policies on race. These attitudes favour treating race issues as implicit rather than explicit and as, in essence, related to some other, more important factors; for example, poverty, social class and suchlike (Kirp, 1981).

Involve parents

Parental encouragement and the educational histories of parents play a crucial role in the aspirations of school students. It is not surprising, and in no way should produce criticism of parents, that if they have been failed by their schooling then they may pass on negative views to their children. HEIs therefore need to work with parents not only to provide information (see Chapter 3) but also to develop and enhance perceptions of HE. In this context, we should note the importance given to links with parents in the evaluation criteria set out in the Ofsted schools inspection framework: 'how well parents are informed and served by the school, and contribute to its life ... the extent to which ... these relationships are used to improve the standards of achievement and the quality of learning' (Ofsted, 1994: 35). In particular, schools are asked to look at the contributions parents make to school life and at the quality of information they provide for parents. There is a variety of possibilities for HEIs here, including taster courses open to parents and children, visits to HE, HE staff having a presence at school career evenings and suchlike. As with raising the aspirations of students, work with parents will need to be gradual and continuous and not some sudden, once-and-for-all, activity which occurs because of some short-term expedient, such as under-recruitment to a particular HE programme.

The rules of the game for school–HE collaboration need to have formal recognition in the structures of schools and HEIs. Only through such formal recognition are resources likely to be maintained. In addition, informal links often make it very difficult to deal with problems which might arise in the operation of collaboration. Even though staff often worry that formalization will take the edge off what are often new and exciting departures, the dangers of not formalizing links are great.

What the school pupils get out of formal collaboration between schools and HEIs is a matter of long-term evaluation, but will include progression to HE for, it is hoped, more black students. HE students ought to get out of this process some form of accreditation and recognition of their work. Schools and HEIs are also likely to benefit from closer links. In purely pragmatic terms, schools, to the extent that more students progress post-16 and post-18, will clearly benefit in terms of league tables and in competition with other schools. There are, however, likely to be more fundamental benefits in terms of school effectiveness and improvement. The emphasis on school effectiveness and improvement might almost be said to be the dominant emphasis in educational practice and research. The work of Sammons *et al.* (1995) is particularly important for us because they argue that schools *do* have an effect, that the effect is located in the organization and structure of the school and that issues of equity are a central plank in any attempt to improve schools. Equity, organization and structure are unlikely to be significantly less important in HEIs, although, as we have been arguing, issues of equity are rarely on HE agendas.

Defining effectiveness in terms of both tests and examination performance and social and affective outcomes associated with attitude and behaviour, Sammons *et al.* identify 11 factors that contribute to the effective school. These include some factors that can be linked to issues of equity and others that could be fostered through links between schools and HEIs. Respect, setting high standards, raising self-esteem, giving pupils positions of authority and having close links with all parents, which are emphasized in school improvement research and practice, are all likely to be best developed where pupils are treated equitably and have access to the full range of opportunities. Underlying these factors is a perspective which challenges ideas that lack of pupil success is the pupil's problem and recognizes that it is the school's. As such, the development of school effectiveness and improvement can help to redress some of the imbalances in opportunities which black students face. Links with HE, including both student tutoring and progression agreements, are likely to have positive effects on at least six of the 11 factors. A shared school vision and shared goals will be enhanced through links with HE which offer progression for those pupils who want it. There are also likely to be knock-on effects in terms of several other factors central to effectiveness and improvement. These include the importance of teaching and learning strategies, high expectations for staff and students, positive reinforcement, home–school partnerships and the school as a learning organization centred upon school-based staff development.

It is not easy to assess the costs of close school–HE relationships, but there are inevitably going to be costs in staff time which will need to be assessed against, for example, the staff and curriculum development benefits of cooperation. The more extensive, Compact-like arrangements are likely to involve costs in terms of coordination, and that is why some have sought support from outside agencies, including Training and Enterprise Councils (TECs) and Education Business Partnerships (EBPs) (Bird and Yee, 1994). Bigger's study of a Compact in Birmingham suggests the benefits and limitations of TEC funding as well as the centrality of positive action in the philosophy of Compacts:

> Post-16 Compact in Birmingham has been targeted on schools and colleges serving inner-city areas where the rate of application to HE was low. These areas are also ethnically mixed, and suffer high unemployment. Compact is marketed as an additional qualification worth credit . . . For those students who are capable of succeeding in HE, this provides the flexibility to compensate for aspects of particular disadvantage, such as operating in English as a second language.
>
> (Bigger, 1996)

There is, however, another dimension to the analysis of the costs and benefits of collaboration which indicates that issues of equity can easily become peripheral. It is important to recognize that although wider access is part of the agendas of both HE and the funding councils, the latter have never rewarded genuine widening of access through funding methodologies. Indeed, funding methodologies for HE have, with the exception of full- and part-time delivery, been neutral as far as types of student are concerned. Neither have the funding councils sought to relate assessments of quality to how successfully HEIs progress diverse groups of students (see Chapter 8). That issues of equity are, as it were, on the back burner in both allocation of funding and assessment of quality provides a perfect reason why HEIs should feel the need to do very little. Recent attempts by the Higher Education Funding Council for England (HEFCE) to deal with issues of disadvantage – for example, by targeted funding to increase access to teacher education for black students – have tended to be short term on the assumption that lessons learned will become part of the mainstream in those institutions successful in getting funding. As suggested here, the problems and the solutions are long term and the solutions may be costly in terms of changes in curriculum design, delivery and assessment. It is, however, worth noting that there are market pressures on HEIs to be more imaginative and flexible in accessing students. These include the likelihood that post-16 staying on rates are at best static, such that the potential numbers of students seeking HE entry may not be expanding.

Having said this, there are, of course, different motivations for school–HE links. The model set out above aims to raise aspirations to HE and is not a mechanism for increasing recruitment to *particular* HEIs. It is for this reason that there are benefits to both schools and HE in developing what might be termed a consortium approach: a number of schools and HEIs working together to develop strategies which enhance aspirations and progression. Within that there will be all sorts of initiatives to recruit to particular institutions and programmes. What has to be avoided is competition between HEIs and schools, which is demanding of time and can often lead to faculties and departments within the same institution not knowing what each are doing in schools 'a', 'b' and 'c'.

This, and the other strategies discussed in subsequent chapters, can be more concisely presented with reference to the *aims* of the strategy, to aspects of *good practice*, to a number of *warnings* and to the *monitoring of outcomes*. As with any checklist of this kind, there are likely to be elements that are more relevant to some localities than to others.

Aims
- Effective, quality links between schools/colleges and HEIs.
- Raised profile of HE and post-16 education, including information on courses available, modes of entry and the nature of the student experience.
- Positive role models for black students, including black men and women.

Good practice
- Consult fully with schools, and offer positive outcomes, e.g. materials.
- Use HE students, in particular black students, as student tutors.
- Recognize and/or accredit HE students' work.
- Relate any activities to the interests of schools and pupils, including careers and post-16 and/or post-19 educational choices.
- Give access to what HE has to offer, rather than developing public relations activities.
- Build on existing consortia (for example, TVEI), or develop consortia of institutions (schools, HE, FE and employers) to operate any system of links.
- For secondary schools, work from year 7 in schools.
- Consider working with primary schools as a means to raise parental aspirations.
- Where the end result is formal school/college/HE Compacts, develop systems of flexible entry which recognize and reward the variety of entry routes.

Warnings
- For HE, don't expect a quick pay-off in terms of recruits.

- For schools and colleges, expect a high demand for these activities.
- Don't forget to involve parents.
- Recognize that the time available for such activities is, for schools and HEIs, limited.

Monitoring outcomes
- Regularly monitor the success of the links and change them if they are not working.
- Set targets for entry to HE institutions/faculties, with annual review.
- Track students regarding progression and experience of HE.
- Regularly feed back information on progression to schools and colleges.

Theoretical and conceptual implications

Discussions about links between schools and HEIs, about consortium approaches to linking and how these relate to black access, raise at least two important theoretical and conceptual issues: the debate about relationships between race and class; and the debate about compensatory, supplementary and separate educational provision.

Race and class

While recognizing that causal explanations in the social sciences are both difficult and contentious, there is a desire for such explanations lying behind much work that has attempted to identify the contributions which race and social class make to educational achievement. There are, of course, really three issues here: what we mean by race and social class; how far the different educational experiences of minorities are related to these two variables; and the essentially political problems involved in attempts to explain racial inequalities in educational underachievement in terms of social class, that is, in terms of class-based material underprivilege.

No attempt will be made here to resolve these issues, and some of the difficulties with the term race have been discussed earlier. However, a number of comments are worth making. With reference to the terms race and class, there is increasing recognition that these should be seen in a non-essentialist way, not as determining how people act and behave but as a variety of ways in which people live their lives and understand their social positions. Race and class are, of course, material and have material consequences, but they are not fixed and immutable. The desire to develop a critique of how these terms have been used is particularly acute in the context of race because race – as an originally biological term – was always highly ideological. In part, the shift from race to ethnicity occurred because of a shift to concerns with lifestyle and culture as ways of identifying minorities, itself the result of a disquiet over the impossibility of linking biological differences to cultural ones. This does not, of course, abolish problems and conflicts. It is one of the features of a new racism, which uses the language of cultural difference, that it uses these cultural issues as bases for discrimination. This is the heart of much of the opposition to black immigration which, it is argued, brings in too much cultural difference! As indicated earlier, there are major problems in identifying cultures and major problems in a cultural absolutism which seeks to identify the essence of a given culture. In particular, such definitions of culture serve to generate fears about other cultures and also tend, through the very emphasis on culture and cultural boundaries, to hide issues of race and racism. As Gillborn (1995: 177) puts it, 'Although current policy discourse makes almost no direct reference to "race", it embodies a familiar line in Conservative political ideology, which supports and extends a racist conception of the "essential" England and the "true" British people.' A similar point is made by Smith (1994): behind discourses on culture and nation lie discourses on race.

Deciding the balance between race and class in educational performance is no less difficult than the similar exercise on the roles of gender and class. In part, the desire to decide which is really significant is a valueless one: black working-class people have always lived their lives with reference to at least race *and* class. In addition, even if the middle-class black person is advantaged materially, there is no evidence that that reduces his or her chances of being racially discriminated against. If racist name-calling in schools occurs regardless of the social class position of the student, then race is a significant variable. It is over this issue that political considerations emerge. First, the attempt to reduce racial inequalities in education to those associated with social class is a far from neutral attempt to say that racial inequalities are not fundamental. This is the case even when we take Gilroy's (1987: 150) point that there is more to the life of black people than race. Second, that same attempt involves a strategy of saying to black people that they are making too much of their ethnicity: too much in the sense that stressing their ethnicity involves a refusal to assimilate and in the sense that these minority ethnicities are, in fact, not discriminated against. Third, that attempt fails to recognize that successful students may be successful despite racial discrimination; put another way, success for black students does not imply that issues of race discrimination have ceased to be significant. Finally, as we will see in Chapter 7, success for many black students in HE does not always translate into equal access to employment opportunities.

Compensatory, supplementary and separate provision

The central argument in this chapter is that we need to pay particular attention to the mainstream when we are talking about black access to higher education. There is, however, a more general debate about which types of educational provision are effective for black people; in particular, about compensatory, supplementary and separate provision. This debate is summed up in the following: 'Because blacks have not always been welcomed in the formal educational system, they have developed ways of learning outside the system. These ways are often creative and culturally relevant' (Sedlacek, 1987: 489).

Compensatory provision is that provision which attempts to make up for failures in the mainstream. An example here would be access courses for black adults who have left school at 16 and have come to realize that they have not reached their potential. Such provision has always been contentious. For some there is a need for dedicated black access courses, while for others such provision should be integrated. For some, such provision has been seen as an easy route into HE. For others, such courses only serve to feed black people into certain occupations where there is a shortage – teaching and social work – and this gives black people a role in policing themselves. Finally, there are those who see the motivations for such courses as being suspect, in that they serve to improve the image of institutions and rarely involve responding to real community needs.

Supplementary provision aims to add to what goes on in the school, because, for example, what is offered there is, for various reasons, inadequate. This inadequacy can be of two kinds: that associated with inadequate delivery of the curriculum, such that a Saturday school might teach more maths and English; and that to do with the absence of some area of study from the curriculum. Here a Saturday school might offer courses in African or Afro-Caribbean history. Only the former is really supplementary, whereas the latter adds something to the educational experience of black students which is absent from mainstream education. As Chevannes and Reeves (1987) argue, what is effectively a black voluntary school movement has primarily involved Afro-Caribbean people, who are the most likely to do badly in mainstream education. Such schools are part-time solutions, with an emphasis on collectivism, strong community involvement and an ethos of solidarity. The curriculum may focus on consciousness raising through courses in African and Afro-Caribbean history, on basic skills in English, maths and sciences, or on a combination of both (Chevannes and Reeves, 1987: 148–55).

Separate education involves an argument for taking groups of students – Afro-Caribbean, Asian, Muslim – out of traditional state schools and establishing separate institutions. The rationale here is that state schooling is not working for these pupils and that, on the analogy with separate schooling for girls, separation might be a route to greater success. The dilemma for both supplementary and separate schooling is, in part, a resource one, in that the state may well not provide funding for either.

There may be dangers to separatism but it is important to recognize that it is a response to a lack of response, to an unwillingness to consider that both structurally and culturally race discrimination adversely affects student performance. The real dangers of separatism are, probably, those demands for separate education for white students which are rooted in a fear of falling academic and cultural standards and are epitomized in the writing of, and debates around, the 'Honeyford affair' (for a summary, see Demaine, 1989, 1993). What is called for in this debate is a form of enclavist and reactive separatism which wishes to maintain an illusory and mythical British identity seen as a key to standards. This suggests that there are different types of, and reasons for, separatism; some – including the call for separate black schools – are reactions to exclusion and attempts to solve it, as well as attempts to create a space in which social and cultural identities can be developed and maintained. Such separatism then becomes a precondition for later inclusion.

Useful texts

Additional material on the debates about race and class and compensatory educational provision can be found in Barker (1981), Gilroy (1987), Miles (1989), Anthias and Yuval-Davis (1992), Troyna (1993), Smith (1994) and Gillborn (1995).

3

Working with Communities, Parents and Students

There is little evidence that HEIs see working with black communities and the dissemination of information specifically to black people as an issue. HE prospectuses provide an interesting case here. Jewson and colleagues (1991), in an analysis of prospectuses, revealed a profoundly ambiguous picture as far as black students are concerned. In terms of text, there were few references to home black students but especial emphasis on provision for overseas students. As they suggest, part of the reason for this is likely to be financial, given the financial incentives to recruit students from outside the UK. In terms of visual images, there is a strong emphasis on HEIs as culturally diverse and ethnically mixed as far as students are concerned, while being mainly white in terms of staffing. As they say, 'ethnic minority candidates who, attracted by the visual images in prospectuses, look more closely for information about the range of facilities and services directed at their needs are likely to be disappointed' (Jewson *et al.*, 1991: 198). In essence, then, prospectuses present a misleading, indeed a false, picture, and easily become a simple exercise in public relations in which the targeted public is the normal, white entrant. While prospectuses are only one form for disseminating information, both the lack of information and its ambiguity are revealed in more detailed studies of the views of black people themselves.

The majority of black students interviewed in the Bath and Bristol study were aware that they and their parents, for whatever reason, lacked information about HE. The difficulties here involve a combination of exclusions: those faced by many white, often working-class, parents who, for a variety of reasons, feel that involvement in school is impossible; and those experienced by many black parents in schools where the majority of parents are white. In both cases, some part of the difficulties relates to parents' own negative experiences of school. However, for some black parents involvement in school is considered to be off the agenda, even though they did progress to further and higher education. This complex of issues in indicated in the following:

My parents just listened to the talk but they don't understand the British system as they were not educated here.

(Abtar, Asian man)

My parents never attended parents evenings ... they were always busy and they had a language problem.

(Nibden, Asian man)

It's not the fault of black parents if they have not had the education themselves.

(Jackie, Afro-Caribbean)

The effect on black pupils here was that they often felt that they progressed through school and into HE without parental support. In large measure, this lack of support was attributed to poor information provided by schools and HEIs, in particular to groups who do not traditionally aspire to HE, and to lack of information in community languages. In the particular case of some Asian parents, there was concern about the nature and appropriateness of higher education for girls:

My dad insisted on Bristol ... my uncle rang [him] and said you cannot let your daughter leave home.

(Shayla, Asian)

My mum was definitely against us leaving home ... life for a home student is different if you have liberal, tolerant parents [but] I don't think it would have worked for me ... basically I lied and told them there were no places in London so when I got the place here [in Bristol] my dad was quite happy.

(Hemlata, Asian woman)

Although many of the issues here relate to the widely recognized point that middle-class parents are more involved than others in school, there are crucial race effects: lack of community language provision, the feeling that HEIs are white institutions, concerns about cultural identity in an HE environment and so on. The important issue here is that black parents were not being blamed for their lack of knowledge and understanding and black cultures were not being pathologized. On the contrary, there was a clear awareness that HEIs could do considerably more to produce and disseminate clear, concise and sensitive material to a wide range of groups whose traditions might not place HE on the agenda.

The commitment to the dissemination of clear, sensitive and impartial material in fact involves the identification of a number of audiences, each with its own concerns. In particular, there will be an audience of parents with children in school who wish to know about higher education; second, there will be an audience which, as potential mature students, is thinking of further study; third, there is an audience, related to the other two but distinct in itself, of people who require materials in community languages. Meeting the needs of these three groups will require consideration of outreach strategies through which information is taken to communities.

Information and its dissemination

A model for the dissemination of information would have to recognize that much of the ignorance about HE and what it has to offer is common to groups of white and black people; put in a slightly different form, there is still a largely middle-class and white ethos within HE and a common perception among those who do not aspire to HE that it is for these same groups of people. 'The kids generally expect us to come in suits, to be posh . . . and just to look down at them and patronize them . . . this guy came up [and] said "I can't believe you're at [university] X"' (black HE interviewee, Bird and Yee, 1994: 16).

Concerns common to white and black people fall into a number of categories: those to do with fitting in, i.e. with fears that HE *is* dominated by clever, articulate people who are not like us; those to do with what HE has to offer and how access happens, i.e. with how far programmes in HE are responsive to student needs in terms of both content and delivery; those to do with finances, including the parental contribution to student maintenance; those to do with survival in HE and progression within it; finally, those associated with career opportunities. However, there is a set of concerns that are specific to black people, whether these be parents of potential HE entrants, school leavers or mature students who themselves aspire to HE, having, for whatever reason, missed out on post-16 education.

For many black parents these concerns relate to issues of race and ethnicity. As indicated in Chapter 2, black school students often face discouragement in school, which includes a systematic avoidance of discussing what HE has to offer. Where parents have experienced school as isolating and discriminatory there is a fear that HE will be similar; that HE will reproduce experiences of name calling and harassment. In addition, there are concerns specific to particular groups of parents; for example, Asian parents are often particularly worried about how daughters will deal with living away from home and how far HE will deny and threaten a cultural heritage. These fears are real to the parents. To deny their reality, even when staff feel that there is no reality to them, is likely to prove problematic. Put another way, tacit knowledge of HE is often based upon ideas which circulate through informal networks of people. Some of this tacit knowledge *is* based upon real fears. The existence and strength of informal networks puts a premium on HE getting it right and suggests that, as a result of black communities often being ignored, trust is difficult to build.

Dissemination of information will, therefore, have to operate on a number of levels: the provision of formal information in a variety of forms (leaflets in English and community languages, video and audio tapes, for example); dissemination of information using both formal and informal channels within local communities (through community centres, schools, religious organizations); strategies to raise the profile of HE within communities (advice centres, taster courses).

Outreach and working with communities

> Lack of consultation with the black community in the past has often
> led to distrust of institutions' intentions when they attempt to establish
> community links . . . collaboration is usually slow to develop and requires
> continuous nurturing and support to establish common ground, under-
> standing and useful working relationships . . . in the early stages of col-
> laboration an intensive investment of staff time and resources may be
> needed from the institution in order to establish a climate of trust.
>
> (UDACE, 1990: 2–3)

Much of what is required in the way of information dissemination is only
possible through what have come to be called outreach strategies. Whereas
FE has a long history of community outreach (FEU/REPLAN, 1989; UDACE,
1990), this is less common in HE, although some aspects of continuing education provision is community-related. The basic problem is that HE is often
distant, both geographically and socially, from black people, so that any
strategy to increase access will have to include taking HE to communities.
This, in itself, requires both an analysis of community needs and an awareness that relationships between black communities and universities are often
both distant and strained.

Even when HE is not geographically distant from black communities it
is often culturally distant. Geographical closeness can, therefore, mask cultural distance. There is often no culture of HE in black communities and
a perception that HE is not for black people. This may be exacerbated by a
history of strained relationships with HE. Therefore, the starting point for
any strategy for working with communities is to build trust and then foster
cooperation. Part of building trust and cooperation will include analysing
and responding to community needs. This is a crucial step because HEIs
cannot assume that what they already have to offer and how they deliver
that provision will meet community needs. Indeed, there is frequently a history of needs analyses in black communities which have not led to positive
responses in terms of provision. Thus the aim of outreach includes 'gathering and collating information on unmet and inappropriately met needs,
and encouraging providers of learning opportunities to respond by development their provision' (REPLAN/NIACE, 1990: 37).

There are, therefore, two steps for HEIs: knowing communities and getting trust. As FEU/FEDA (1995) indicates, community profiling is an essential prerequisite for any education institution which wants to meet community
needs, as profiling will yield the basic statistical picture of communities on
which policies and practices can be based. The great potential advantage
for HEIs is that the data from the 1991 Census are available on CD-ROM
and can provide a great deal of ethnic data by census enumeration district,
electoral ward and county. These data include, for example, statistics on
ethnic groups in the total population and the age profiles of ethnic groups.
These data can provide a basis for seeing, for example, whether black students

from local communities access the full range of HE provision, what types of delivery are appropriate and which make provision accessible.

The steps to building trust and cooperation and analysing and responding to needs are often difficult to take because of past and present barriers. As UDACE (1990: 25–6) suggests, barriers include suspicion concerning the motives and seriousness of educational institutions; the absence of black people in senior positions in education; fears that education institutions are linking with communities for their own private and dubious motives; differences in principles and working styles; and lack of resources and staff time in community organizations. Alongside these barriers is an often total lack of knowledge in HE of what community organizations exist and how they operate.

Working with communities includes identifying and responding to needs, while recognizing that there may be a multiplicity of community organizations in an area. That multiplicity can, itself, pose problems for HE. It may provide a justification for not working with communities at all, either because the multiplicity of organizations and groups makes such work difficult or because of stereotypical views that the mutiplicity indicates something about the lack of focus in black communities. Alternatively, HEIs may choose to work with one or two larger community organizations which they see, rightly or wrongly, as representative. This is automatically going to exclude many smaller community groups. Outreach also involves recognizing that there is a range of client groups. School pupils are probably catered for in their schools; adults, however, may have little provision and, to the extent that many are parents, that lack of access to provision may have a negative effect on children's aspirations. For adults, therefore, there is the need for not only particular programmes, but also programmes delivered in a particular way and in a particular environment. FEU/REPLAN (1989: 25–6) indicated, in looking at provision up to FE level, that adults want flexible and modularized programmes in the community; that is, in community centres and in schools. They also want high quality provision that has parity of esteem with that offered in FE. In terms of curriculum and delivery, the most important issues are: equality between tutors and students, the very opposite of much past educational experience; curriculum content and delivery that is negotiated; a curriculum that is modularized, with self-standing units that can be accredited individually; and a curriculum that offers opportunities for progression. It is unlikely that the requirements for HE in and by black communities would be markedly different.

HE provision in the community could therefore include programmes to increase awareness of what is on offer: HE taster courses, HE experience modules and activities, as well as joint programmes, including access programmes, with FE and adult education provision for those without the right qualifications for HE entry. In addition, HEIs could develop systems through which some aspects of HE programmes are delivered in communities. There are at least two possibilities here: for HE staff to teach in the community and for HE to franchise provision to other providers, including FE colleges and community organizations. Issues of resourcing and quality assurance and control are likely to favour FE franchising, which may have the additional advantage that FEIs are often more accessible to black people than HEIs. Although there is a variety of systems of collaboration between HE and FE which involve providing HE programmes closer to local communities (these involve some 50,000 students), the majority do not, as yet, target black students (Bird *et al.*, 1993). There is a difficulty in community provision in that fears of its quality have been widespread (see, for example, 'Second class degree risk', *Times Higher Educational Supplement*, 29 April 1994) and, whether these fears are well-founded or not, they are likely to discourage potential students from taking advantage of forms of delivery which *are* often more flexible and responsive than those offered on campus.

Information dissemination and flows

> He cycled around for an hour before coming in the door . . . there was clearly tremendous anxiety about coming and discussing education.
> (Bird *et al.*, 1992a: unpublished transcript)

This is a description of a situation at an event in a local black community which was targeting mature students for entry to HE. The Afro-Caribbean man found great difficulty in entering the building, even though it was a building designed as a community centre for black people. The lesson is not so much one about how to work in communities as discussed above, but is to do with information and how it is disseminated. However good the publicity, however much it is translated into community languages, however welcoming the environment, for many potential students higher education is very far from their minds; it has, as indicated earlier, been erased from their agendas during compulsory schooling.

Information therefore needs to be relevant, accessible, impartial and delivered at the right point. Relevance includes community language provision and, in addition, the extent to which provision has responded to community needs. Neither of these is either simple to guarantee or customary. Typically, universities will do a quick sweep of an area, flooding it with information about what has always been available. As such, the dissemination is producer- rather than client-orientated and takes an existing portfolio of provision and offers that to a new client group. Less commonly, universities will have a regular community presence in, for example, community centres and schools or in some community-based guidance centre, with regularly available information. This latter is likely to be more successful, as it will favour the development of networks of people who can cascade the knowledge of HE to their friends and peers. It is only *more* likely to be effective, and is no guarantee of success. There is often a reasonable concern that it is the lack of accessibility of local universities in the past which makes new channels of communication and new sources of information ineffective.

Where community language provision in considered it is often in a simplistic manner: translate information and that is all we need to do. That there is more to do is, with a little insight, clear. It is, for example, generally most effective to give the job of translation to local community facilities as this will, in itself, form part of outreach activity. In addition, it is not always effective to provide translated materials in a community language on its own. For example, if a leaflet is translated into Urdu, then it will often go to a family where several or all members are fluent in English. Not including English *and* Urdu versions on the same leaflet can be seen as patronizing. Finally, there is little point in having leaflets in community languages if, at the stage of enquiring to HE, there is no such provision. Setting up expectations that, at all levels, community language speakers will be available, and then not having them on the end of telephones during the summer, when students and often parents want to enquire about entry to HE, is likely to increase perceptions of the distance and lack of accessibility of HE.

We can illustrate several of these issues by taking two examples of working with black communities, one involving a university, the other an Open College Network (see UDACE, 1990, for more details). The then Lancashire Polytechnic (now University of Central Lancashire) identified under-representation of Asian and Afro-Caribbean people in the institution. Working with an umbrella community organization, the Community Relations Council, it recommended and had established a Race Equality Unit, funded through Section 11. Formal and informal systems developed. Formal ones included an internal advisory committee involving academic, support and service staff and students and an external advisory committee which included representatives of 20 ethnic minority community organizations. The main purposes of the formal system were to identify black community needs and assist in the development of race equality policy in the institution. This policy included systems through which black students could, via the Race Equality Unit, express their views and discuss their experiences. An informal set of links between the Race Equality Unit and a wide range of black individuals and organizations was also established. This system provided support for local black groups, linked staff with black people in the community and encouraged black community groups to use HE facilities. The unit also organized seminars on a range of issues, including ethnic monitoring, women in Bangladesh and black politicians in the UK. The success of these initiatives is indicated in increased recruitment of black students (for example, 25 per cent more Asian entrants in 1989 than in 1988), in the increasing awareness within the institution of issues of race equality and in a higher profile for the institution in black communities. Similar success was evident in work with a targeted Yemeni community by the South Yorkshire Open College Federation. Following work primarily on literacy levels, not only were Yemeni literacy assistants identified, trained and accredited within the community, but there was an increased participation within the Yemeni community in post-compulsory education and training, including entry to HE.

The lessons of both these initiatives include the importance of community-based needs analysis, the development of a wide spectrum of provision on the basis of that analysis and the development of systems of accreditation for those involved. Included in such responsiveness is the need for advocacy for those who may lack either experience or confidence in dealing with HEIs, where advocacy includes 'negotiating directly with institutions or agencies on behalf of individuals or groups for whom there may be additional barriers to access or to learning' (REPLAN/NIACE, 1990: 38).

There is a model for such wide-spectrum, community-based provision in the American community college system (FEFC, 1995). They provide a full range of provision from short vocationally based courses up to the first two years of degrees, and do this in facilities that are available all year round and for seven days a week. Additional advantages include a full range of preparatory courses available to students who may enter college with no formal qualifications and no idea of what they wish to do. In consequence, there are well developed and well resourced systems of guidance and counselling which include necessary advocacy.

If we recognize that many groups of black people have had negative experiences of compulsory education and that some of these negative experiences are passed from parents to children, it is not surprising that strategies for linking with black communities are difficult to set up and are often viewed with mistrust. This is why the setting up of such links is important if access is to be increased for black people but also why many strategies for community links either fail or take considerable time to come to fruition. In essence, disseminating information about HE and delivering HE provision in communities is neither a quick fix nor inexpensive. Resistance to resourcing such provision is, in the end, about the triumph of short-termism if for no other reason than that increasingly HEIs will have to recruit from their local communities and catchment areas.

Recognizing the difficulties discussed above, we can again identify *aims*, *good practice*, a set of *warnings* and *monitoring of outcomes*.

Aims
- An increase in information about HE, including about courses, entry requirements and employment opportunities.
- Effective and accessible information on HE.
- Information which meets the needs of a wide variety of clients.
- The development of HE provision in communities.

Good practice
- Involve local black community groups.
- Make information sensitive to the needs and interests of black community groups.
- Make information user-friendly: use question and answer formats, for example.
- For any piece of information material, always include a community language and an English version together.

- Distribute information free and widely.
- Include in information useful addresses, contact people and phone numbers.
- Develop a community presence (community centres, festivals, etc.) and have black staff involved in that activity.
- Develop HE provision in the community which is based upon the basic principles of *negotiation, equality, modularization* and *progression,* and is high quality.

Warnings
- Raising expectations that are not met, including the non-availability, in HEIs, of speakers of community languages to give immediate advice, may inhibit access.
- Omitting English language text from leaflets is potentially, and often actually, patronizing.
- Be aware, as an HEI, that the provision you offer may not meet the needs of communities seeking entry to HE.
- Expect resistance, especially where you have never been in communities before and where HEIs have a negative image in communities.
- Recognize that the quality of community provision is essential and that it will be expensive.

Monitoring outcomes
- Track students from initial contact with community provision.

Theoretical and conceptual implications

With regard to dissemination of information and working with communities, while it is true that many black parents feel alienated from the education system in much the same way as do many white working-class parents, we would also have to argue that this alienation has to do with something other than – and in addition to – social class. In particular, this alienation is often related precisely to issues of race discrimination and harassment within education. There are, therefore, two issues that are important: the role that culture plays in attitudes to education, and related debates about assimilation and integration.

Culture and education

The recognition that certain groups are less interested in education is, in part, to do with culture and history. In addition, the fact that parents may, for example, resist their daughter's leaving home to study in university is again a cultural issue. However, there is a number of problems in seeking a cultural explanation for attitudes to education. First, cultures are embedded in structures and histories, structures and histories which may have excluded children from full participation in the education system. As such, those histories are as much structural as cultural, and include structures of discrimination which operate regardless of people's culture. Second, cultures do not exist in a vacuum but in relationship to, and often in contestation with, other cultures. If culture is a significant variable in determining attitudes to education, then the culture of educational institutions is likely to be as important as the culture of parents and children. This is part of the reason why it is crucial to recognize that education institutions do have an effect on students within them; that is, that cultures outside education are not all-powerful and all-determining. Third, it is very easy to see cultures which include resistance to education in negative terms and to pathologize them. This is likely to be the case where the structural context – including race discrimination – is ignored and where the understanding of other cultures is based upon stereotypes. Finally, if the problem is seen as cultural then a cultural solution to it is likely to be identified, one which may often seek to devalue some culture or another. If the culture of home and of school, college or university clash, then something has to change. 'Change your home culture and your children will succeed' might well be the maxim. It is, however, part of Taylor's argument (Taylor and Gutmann, 1992), and is explicit in discussion of equality assurance (Runnymede Trust, 1993), that the variety of cultures should receive recognition, including recognition in the education system. One of the aims of equality assurance *is* recognition: 'to support the development of cultural and personal identities' (Runnymede Trust, 1993). The important point here is that identity is in the plural. The implication is that there should not be a hegemonic culture within education, a curriculum which is national in the narrow, particular and exclusionary sense.

That developing strategies to give equality of recognition to a diversity of cultures is not an end in itself, or a panacea, is clear. As argued above, knowing about other people's cultures and ways of life is no guarantee of acceptance and recognition and may, indeed, increase levels of discrimination and intolerance. However, ignorance of other cultures is sure to produce a lack of recognition and will provide no basis for challenging misconceptions and stereotypes.

Assimilation, integration and pluralism

In policy terms, the debate about the recognition of diverse cultures and how this affects strategies for working with black communities relates to debates about assimilation, integration and pluralism. As Troyna (1993) argues, these policies have a complex and highly politicized history. As a policy, assimilation involves a process in which one culture is seen as dominant and in which all those who hold to minority cultures should give them up, should assimilate. Assimilationism is profoundly asymmetrical, for it involves loss if you are someone from a minority culture (Troyna, 1993: 23). In addition, assimilationism assumes that the identification of the dominant culture is unproblematic and that this culture is uncontested and unitary. Assimilation is then seen as not only a condition for educational success but also as a condition for becoming British, even though the precise meaning of British is left indeterminate. Assimilationism therefore has a profoundly orientalist tone (Said, 1978), in that it continually contrasts 'our' culture with all its benefits and positive features to 'their' culture with all its deficits and negativities. As such, assimilationism is monocultural and includes a claim that 'our' culture is easily identifiable and homogeneous.

Integration and integrationism in some sense came after, and responded to, policies based on assimilation. Whereas the latter denied the validity of other cultures, the former used the language of equal opportunity, of cultural diversity and of tolerance. The aim was to enhance minority achievement, depressed because of assumed low self-esteem, by valuing the range of cultures and, in so doing, to produce racial and ethnic tolerance. As Troyna and Carrington (1990: 20) argue, 'The focus of concern was cultural differences and the extent to which these were regarded as inhibiting the educational careers and experiences of black students . . . there was a determination to ensure that the lifestyles of black pupils were reflected (and respected) in curriculum models and teaching schemes.' It is this same position, usually called multiculturalism or cultural pluralism, that was criticized by Stone (1980) on the grounds not only that evidence for low black self-esteem was dubious, but also that inserting multiculturalism into schools detracted from the core of the curriculum. Her point was also that black parents want mainstream education and not what Troyna and others came to call the three S's approach of saris, samosas and steel bands (Troyna and Carrington, 1990: 20). Cultural pluralism involved the assertion that understanding culture was a route to success but, in so doing, led to an almost total lack of consideration of structural issues; that is, racist structures inside and outside school.

The critique of integrationism and cultural pluralism saw the emergence of anti-racist education, which not only emphasized the significance of what happens outside the school in terms of what was termed institutional racism but also stressed the significance of teacher racism. In political terms this included a healthy scepticism about how far education can compensate for society and sometimes to a call for separate education for black people (see Chapter 2).

These policies had their heydays: assimilationism in the 1960s and 1970s, integrationism and pluralism in the 1980s. There is, however, another trend in educational policy which has also matched wider changes in politics generally, and that is deracialization. In essence, this involves a return to a form of assimilationism. This deracialization involves three processes: talking about something else instead of issues of race, in particular talking about nation, culture and way of life, all of which are characterized as unitary; reducing issues of race to something else, such as inner-city problems, poverty and unemployment; refusing to see race as anything other than the prejudices of a small minority, i.e. as lacking any structural components. The implications here are that race is not a policy issue at all and that those who assert that it is are probably doing so mischievously. Further, deracialization allows racist attitudes to be expressed quite openly. Gillborn (1995: 30) cites a telling example of this in which a white parent rejected a school where the majority were of Pakistani origin. The parent wanted a majority of white friends for her child and did not want her child to come home singing Pakistani songs or to learn this particular foreign language. As Gillborn (1995: 30) says, 'This is perhaps the most dangerous consequence of spurious deracialization. The ability to deny "race" any legitimacy in a debate, and thereby to leave the way clear for practices that have racist consequences, regardless of their deracialized facade.'

Useful texts

Additional material on the debates about cultural and structural factors, and the variety of policy positions, can be found in Cashmore and Troyna (1988), Troyna and Carrington (1990), Rattansi (1992), Miles (1993), Troyna (1993) and Gillborn (1995).

Part 2

Strategies for Quality and Equality in Higher Education

Part of the aim of this book is to redress the balance in the discussion of how black people do in the race for higher education and to emphasize how they progress through HE as much as how they gain access to HE in the first place. Chapters 2 and 3 were, therefore, devoted to issues of access and identified the importance of working with schools, as that is the mainstream from which black people are either going to progress successfully to HE or are going to fail to progress, often for reasons associated with the quality of schooling. In addition, clear deficits in the nature and quality of information available to black people were identified. Strategies for working with schools, for disseminating information and linking HE with black communities may all serve to increase the demand from black people for places in HE.

However, we still need to know and understand what happens to black students in HE, be they ones who have entered at 18 through school and/ or FE or those who, as adults, have taken access, Open College and other programmes which make up for deficits in schooling. In essence, the issues for Chapters 4 and 5 are the quality of the black student experience in HE and how staff and curriculum development initiatives and the establishment of black support groups can enhance quality.

4

Staff and Curriculum Development in Higher Education

You are getting white people talking and lecturing about racism and yet they won't confront their own racism.

(Billy, Afro-Caribbean)

One of the lecturers was watching everything this [black] guy was doing ... he was having problems with one of the subjects ... and it was anything that he did; he was waiting to kick him off the course.

(Yvonne, Afro-Caribbean)

As far as I was concerned ... I was taught black people didn't have a history ... I was taught about the Egyptians at school but I wasn't taught [they] were black; I was taught they were somebody from the moon or something.

(Tahseen, Asian woman)

It's not the problem of black people, it's the problem of white people ... Trying to change people's views is extremely hard.

(Delroy, Afro-Caribbean)

There was a strongly held view among the overwhelming majority of the black students in the Bath and Bristol study that the attitudes of staff – usually white staff – were causing them problems. These problems related to a range of factors, including how black students were treated by staff and how curricula were designed and delivered. From the point of view of white staff – as indicated in Chapter 1 – there were equally strongly held views that, for example, discrimination was a rarity and curricula were sacrosanct and could not be altered in order to respond to the diversity of students. These issues served to exacerbate the isolation of black students, to produce senses of grievance and, potentially, to affect progression. In addition, many black students felt that relationships with staff were made more difficult because of the lack of black staff in HE and that relationships with white students were also often strained.

There is no clear evidence that the attitudes and behaviours of white staff and students are affecting, for example, degree performance in HE. Indeed, there is little research into this issue, in part because of the privileging of issues of access over those of progression. While this lack of research leaves the relationship between the performance of black students and the influence of student and staff attitudes indeterminate, it is still the case that these attitudes are, for those black students, affecting the quality of the student experience. In other words, black students may perform well while simultaneously experiencing HE as a very negative process. This has important implications for assessment of the quality of the student experience and, clearly, any measures which only look at the output from higher education would miss the dimension of on-course experiences. Equally, however, it may prove difficult, in an institution where black students feel disempowered and are suspicious of the motives of white staff and students, to get evidence of those aspects of the students' experience which relate to discrimination.

Background

In general terms, as Brown and Sommerlad (1992) argue, the position of staff development in HE is equivocal. Leaving aside that element of staff development which is related to research, they characterize staff development in universities in the following terms. It is event-driven, rather than focusing on more process forms of development. It sees training as a solution to problems, even though there is little follow-up to see if training works. It is remedial and thus implies a deficit model of staff skills and competencies. It is voluntaristic and therefore involves only those who are already committed. In addition, it is under- or unresourced, usually peripheral to other things and frequently technical: how to use a computer, how to use the Internet (Brown and Sommerlad, 1992: 184–6). Therefore, except in a small number of department and faculties, including education, which have a culture of continuing professional development, it has little relationship to the continuing professional development of academic and support staff and makes little contribution to making HEIs into learning organizations.

As far as staff and curriculum development work which focuses on race and ethnic diversity is concerned, considerable work has already been carried out in FE and schools. This includes a wide range of work done by the FEU (1986a, b, c, d, 1987a, b, 1989). In addition, the Ofsted guidelines for the inspection of schools (1994) include explicit references to how schools deal with issues of racial diversity in school management and in teaching, learning and assessment. These particular issues have received considerably less attention in higher education for reasons which will be explored below.

Organization

In order to respond to some of the concerns of black students outlined above, a series of staff and curriculum development sessions was arranged for the three HEIs involved in the Bath and Bristol study, focusing on issues of ethnic diversity in higher education. The aim was to develop a structured but flexible programme of staff and curriculum development which would tackle issues of race and ethnic diversity in HE. An initial pilot in one institution – to identify the needs of staff and the appropriate ways to respond – was followed by four sessions involving the three HEIs. A final session was arranged for senior management in one of the HEIs. In large measure, this final session resulted from the lack of senior management involvement in the earlier sessions. All sessions were facilitated by experienced trainers – in this case, black trainers – from outside the institutions involved. A maximum number of participants was set at 25, with, as far as possible, equal numbers from each HEI, and the venue was rotated around the institutions. Heads of department/faculty were contacted to nominate participants, and it was emphasized that attendance should be voluntary. While it was recognized that making attendance voluntary would pre-select a group of committed staff, the intention was to train such staff, who could then become, in their departments, faculties and institutions, centres for the dissemination of good practice. The trainers took the view that making attendance compulsory would, at this developmental stage, threaten the viability and success of the whole exercise. The intention was that those who had volunteered for training would disseminate findings in their institutions; good practice would cascade through those institutions even though, of course, any radical resistance would not be tackled by this method. The problem of staff who are radically opposed to such staff and curriculum development was not addressed.

Structure

The programme of sessions covered the following areas: the background to discussions of diversity; access and admissions policies; curriculum issues; and ethnic monitoring.

Clearing the ground

It was recognized that, despite the attendance by staff who were already sympathetic to issues of ethnic diversity, they would start from different levels of understanding and experience. Part of this initial session aimed to assess people's understanding and experience and to use those with more expertise to assist those with less. Issues of race were also tackled indirectly: they were, for example, introduced through discussions of gender – getting women and men in the group to discuss their experiences of discrimination and then generalizing this discussion to include race discrimination. The emphasis was therefore on sensitivity and indirection. Indirection was favoured in order to introduce issues in terms of things with which the participants were familiar. As many of them had considerable experience of gender relations in the workplace and little of black–white relationships, gender issues provided a useful starting point and a basis for moving on to discussions of race and racism. Sensitivity is likely to be good practice for all staff and curriculum development, in that it is a means to build trust. Race issues, where there are often strongly held, emotionally charged and negative views, require especially delicate handling. Indirection and sensitivity are not rooted in a desire to go easy on issues of discrimination, but in the recognition that heavy-handedness may exacerbate existing feelings of defensiveness and anxiety in white people.

Ground clearing was also important in a number of other senses: in allowing people to discuss sensitive issues in a non-threatening context; in allowing them to clarify basic conceptual issues, such as what is meant by 'race', by 'ethnicity', by 'black' and so on; in outlining some of the legal ground, such as the essential aspects of the 1976 Race Relations Act; in facilitating discussions of the distinction between direct and indirect discrimination, and how this distinction could be applied in HE to the situation of black students. What became clear in this attempt to clear the ground was that many staff were, in fact, uncertain about both the conceptual and terminological issues and also about the nature and content of existing legislation.

For this, and for the other three sessions, a combination of inputs was used: inputs by the trainers, e.g. on the legal position concerning equal opportunities policies and positive action programmes; the provision and discussion of materials, e.g. on HE admissions figures and what these tell us about the representation of black people; workshops on developing admissions policies and policies on racial harassment; planning sessions to identify what staff could do in their institutions in both the short and long terms.

Access and admissions

The primary focus of this session was on the sorts of strategy which could increase the entry of black students into HE, with particular emphasis on outreach activities and the formulation and use of admissions policies at institutional and departmental/faculty levels. Neither of these had become part of how the three HEIs actually operated. None had formally developed admissions policies and none had consistently used outreach. Indeed, where outreach had been developed it had been unsuccessful in terms of what staff expected, i.e. in recruiting students to particular HE programmes. In this sense, staff had a pragmatic and short-term view of outreach, which contrasts with the realities of effective outreach discussed in Chapter 3.

One particular emphasis was on the different rates of admission for different groups of black students and how these could be tackled, in particular with a view to increasing access for those who are most under-represented; that is, Afro-Caribbean and Bangladeshi students. Perhaps the most important aspect of admission policies is the setting of targets for recruitment; it is only with targets that the effectiveness of such policies can be evaluated and reviewed. It became clear in these sessions that effective admissions policies, with appropriate recruitment targets, would have to be backed by institutional support and, probably, financial incentives for the meeting of targets. In addition, it became clear that admissions targets were only a small part of an effective strategy to widen access. Staff were well aware that a multi-agency approach involving schools, FE colleges, local communities and other organizations was essential. They were equally well aware that such approaches were rare and that, for many HEIs, there was a very equivocal reaction to strategies to widen access, especially where these were targeting local black students.

The development of such policies had proved difficult in several institutions, in part because of misunderstanding about the purposes and methods of targeting, and in part for a range of politico-resource reasons. There were major confusions between targeting and the setting of quotas, the former being legal under the 1976 Race Relations Act, the latter not; many of those who opposed targeting were also concerned with what they saw as lowering of standards. There were strong feelings, against all the evidence, that target setting *requires*, for example, some relaxation of entry requirements in order to access black students. The confusion here was exacerbated by confusion about what is meant by flexible entry to HE, with flexibility still regularly being perceived as the devaluation of GCE A levels or the trading off of A levels for other, less important qualifications. There was, in fact, a major division of opinion between City Polytechnic and City College of HE staff on the one hand and those from City University on the other. The latter were more convinced of the value of GCE A levels than the former and, therefore, were less convinced of the value of alternative entry criteria. In part this difference related to the missions of the institutions and to the self-perceptions of the staff: polytechnic and college staff saw the importance of local access and the primacy of teaching, whereas university staff saw their student market as national and international and one of their primary missions as quality research.

The access and admissions session therefore set out not only to clarify the nature of targeting but also to provide information on the achievements of black students in schools and FE. In addition, some outreach strategies were identified (see Chapter 3). Politico-resource issues were also addressed. Departmental/faculty staff were uneasy about rewards; for example, in the form of top-sliced monies being allocated to successful faculties, in particular the extent to which certain departments/faculties would benefit to the exclusion of others. Again, evidence was presented and discussed to show: (a) that where institutions had attempted to reward success in widening access, this had rarely worked to the major disadvantage of individual faculties, especially where good practice developed in one faculty could be used, in the future, by another; and (b) the importance of an institutional commitment to policy formation in the area of admissions. Discussion also focused on the different cultures of HEIs. Clearly, those with more central-ized control of budgets will find it easier to establish systems of financial rewards for meeting admissions targets than those with budgetary devolu-tion. This will be particularly important where there is resistance to target-ing and rewards. Perhaps the crucial issue here is that institutions have an obligation to operate fair and equitable admissions policies and practices, and therefore that they need to be aware how such policies and practices can become covertly unfair. As indicated elsewhere in this book, the *poten-tial* for indirect discrimination may, in fact, be very great.

Curriculum issues

The assumption was made in this session that curricula were not sacro-sanct and that issues of ethnic diversity have important consequences for the design, content, delivery and assessment of programmes/modules. It was recognized that HEIs have greater discretion in curriculum design, delivery and assessment than either schools or FE colleges and therefore have less of an excuse for curricula which lack responsiveness to the diversity of stu-dents. Some of the staff involved already had some experience of such cur-riculum development work and the seemingly inevitable resistance to it.

There was considerable unease about relationships between the curric-ulum and ethnic diversity and also a very narrow conception of the curric-ulum which focused on content. Many participants came close to the view discussed by McCarthy (1994: 11): they 'have stressed attitudinal models of reform . . . [and] have tended to paste over the central contradictions associated with race and the curriculum, promoting instead a professional discourse of content addition.' The solution becomes one in which some content is added to a course, or a course dedicated to issues of ethnic diversity is developed. In both these cases something develops which is remarkably like multicultural education in schools, in that it sees the issue as one of responding to cultural diversity. To counter this, and broaden concerns, some ideas developed in work by the FEU formed the basis for the session(s) (FEU, 1989, Volume 3).

1. The basic principle behind curriculum innovation is that *all* students should learn about ethnic diversity as an integral part of their education. This would apply even in those institutions which have very few, if any, black students. However, it has to be recognized that students brought up with racist views cannot view other cultures as equal and may react to information about diversity in a racist fashion. This then raises the issue, which is discussed later, of how we deal with racism both in policy terms and through staff and curriculum development.

2. The curriculum includes not only content, but delivery, assessment, aspects of classroom interaction and support services; that is, a whole learning environment. This is why a narrow view of the curriculum and a narrow curriculum solution are likely to be inadequate.

3. Curricula do not, therefore, stand alone, so seeking to make them more responsive to diversity is likely to fail if there is race discrimination in the institution; for example, in student and/or staff recruitment.
4. Tackling diversity in the curriculum must include looking not only at other cultures but also at the racial inequalities which members of such cultures regularly face. This forms the heart of a possible distinction between multicultural and multiracial issues: the former dealing with aspects of the culture of different groups, the latter with the structures of discrimination faced by those groups.
5. Finally, from the students' perspective, any innovation in the curriculum should empower them through building their experiences into programmes/modules. This is particularly important for black students, who often see curricula as not referring to their experience and as lacking any reference to their, albeit hidden and silenced, histories.

The starting point, therefore, for any innovations in curricula will be a curriculum audit of the department/faculty, which will imply more general audits of the institution with reference to the full range of equal opportunities issues. As with many policy developments of this kind, it is easier for a department/faculty to innovate if the ethos of the institution is supportive. Such an ethos will obviously include a positive encouragement of equity and positive discouragement of discriminatory practices and attitudes.

Curriculum innovation can involve three related strategies: first, dealing with what are essentially cultural issues (here we could include reference to works by black academics who are often excluded); second, introducing structural issues, so that evidence of race discrimination would be included in a variety of curricula; finally – and as an extension of the second – having race as an issue in all courses, rather than having specific courses dedicated to race issues. These innovations will be less successful where the environment outside the course is still characterized by discrimination and exclusion. What may seem trivial to a white member of staff or students – spelling or pronouncing someone's name incorrectly, treating that name as odd or humorous – may be serious for a black student.

Ethnic monitoring

The point of this session was to make the distinction between *ethnic enumeration,* i.e. counting of students on entry to and exit from courses, and *ethnic monitoring,* which includes tracking students through their courses and into employment, and eliciting qualitative data on their experiences. Ethnic monitoring, in this sense, becomes a crucial adjunct of effective admissions policies, and indicates an institutional commitment to doing more than simply opening the doors to HE. The emphasis on monitoring links this activity to measures of the quality of the student experience, measurements which must be quantitative and qualitative (see Chapter 6).

Participants must be enabled to link what they learn in the sessions to their places of work. It is for this reason that they were asked to identify short- and long-term objectives for them in the context of their institution and their position within it. The range of objectives was very wide and included: increasing links with black communities; increasing numbers of black staff in HE; examining one's own prejudices; scrutinizing courses/modules and teaching styles with regard to ethnic diversity; monitoring the performance of *all* students, i.e. not singling out black students; developing admissions policies; extending staff development sessions to non-academic staff; building staff and curriculum development sessions dealing with ethnic diversity into the existing system of staff and curriculum development. Therefore, the participants were moving beyond the typical model discussed by Brown and Sommerlad (1992), towards an awareness that staff and curriculum development needs to be fully integrated into HE provision. Significantly, many of the concerns which were stressed in short- and long-term plans related to admissions or staffing, and mainly academic staff; there was little concern, on the face of it, with white students or with support staff. Indeed, the lack of a focus on white students was, in part, a way of avoiding a crucial problem; that is, that many black students were aware of discrimination by those students. Given that the majority of interaction for students is with other students, both in and outside classes, then the need for work with students is perhaps greater than for that with staff. Only in certain faculties – particularly social work and health – had issues of student attitudes and behaviour been tackled, in part because of strong lobbying by black student support groups (see Chapter 5). As might be expected, tackling students' attitudes and behaviour proved explosive, in particular because these were addressed in mixed groups of black and white students. Two ideal typical group situations developed, neither of which was the basis for constructive discussion and change. In the first, white students said virtually nothing when faced with the fact of black students recounting experiences of discrimination. They were clearly intimidated, anxious and guilty, but were unable to respond. In the second, white students responded to evidence of discrimination in a hostile, often racist, fashion.

Where student attitudes have become an issue for discussion and innovation, the attempt can be made to establish contracts with white students that discriminatory attitudes and behaviours will, as far as possible, be excluded from the lecture and seminar situations. There is, of course, a strongly inimical political climate to such contracting, which easily reduces the attempt to develop civility in the classroom to issues of political correctness. One attempt to develop such a contract on a module dedicated to issues of race and ethnicity produced some hostile reaction from white students, including the claim that staff 'are trying to control what we can say' (unpublished transcript). This was a reaction to what staff saw as a perfectly reasonable attempt to exclude some terms – coloured and half caste being the least unacceptable – from the learning environment. Perhaps the lesson here is that we should not assume that white students who enter HE are, because of their educational histories and backgrounds, free from attitudes and behaviours that offend.

Such contracts do not, of course, address the issues of interaction outside the teaching space, or deal with situations where the contracts fail to be effective. Although institutions have policies to tackle abusive behaviour and language, their effectiveness is rarely measured and they often have in-built problems. One example would be the need for the victim of abuse to complain. Black students in a largely white institution may find it difficult to complain of abuse for good reasons, which include the fear of retaliation and the lack of black people to whom to complain. The heart of this issue is the extent to which policy is reactive or proactive; the extent to which an institution reacts to incidents of racial harassment or is more proactive in making it clear, through, for example, clear and effective disciplinary procedures, that racial harassment is out of order. The issue here is also the wider one of the difference between having a policy and having an ethos in which that policy is effectively applied and its applications are monitored.

What was significant was that in none of the institutions studied had ethnic diversity been seen as an appropriate issue for staff and curriculum development work; a small number of faculties and departments had established their own strategies, but these had rarely influenced the wider institutional context. As in many other HEIs, staff development was seen as primarily research focused, to do with the publication of scholarly articles and the gaining of research grants, monies and rankings. Staff and curriculum development focused on teaching was of less significance and when it did occur was centred on issues associated with increasing student numbers rather than issues of diversity. The central concern was not meeting the needs of a diversity of students – which includes a recognition that diverse students may have diverse needs – but how to deal with greater student numbers, with more marking and suchlike. It is noticeable that the protocols for HEFCE teaching quality assessment (HEFCE, 1995) do not include any direct references to ethnic diversity and that assessor training makes little, if any, reference to ethnic diversity (see Chapter 8 below for further discussion). In summary, for many staff in HE, there was a hierarchy of staff and curriculum development activities. First, there are those activities which focus on research and publications. Second, where teaching is seen as important, development deals with managerial issues, such as assessing large numbers of students, rather than policy issues. Lastly, where policy issues are on the agenda they are mission driven and, given that missions often emphasize access, staff development is similarly focused on this issue.

It is worth emphasizing the distinctiveness of the session involving 12 senior managers, including heads of department, members of the directorate and senior administrative staff. Senior management had been absent from the previous sessions for a combination of reasons: they saw the session as focused on teaching staff and saw themselves as merely brokers who were making the sessions possible. However, teaching staff themselves were highly critical of their absence and that was one of several reasons – including the importance of ethos and resources, which need a lead from senior management – for having a dedicated session for them.

Senior management seemed to be no more aware of the legal background to race issues than were academic staff. They were, however, much more ready to raise resource constraints as a basis for saying that there are severe restrictions on what institutions can do. Comprehensive monitoring of students was seen as desirable but difficult because of resource and database constraints. Within the session, there also seemed to be a link between the reliance on resource and technical objections to, for example, monitoring and the training itself. In essence, the objections were being rationalized as a way of not accepting what the black trainers were suggesting. The unease about having black trainers who are, as it were, 'telling it like it is' was dealt with by a resort to resource and technical arguments. In other words, while the objections were real as far as senior management was concerned, they also allowed management to say simultaneously, 'We are doing what we can but not as much as you, the trainers, claim is needed.'

The lack of awareness of the legal framework as it impacts on HE and the willingness to resort to resource arguments are, of course, linked in a potentially explosive fashion. In particular, HEIs have no more right to discriminate on grounds of ethnicity than other employers, but the lack of awareness of the legal framework makes the possibility of unintentional unequal treatment all the greater. Only by resourcing monitoring can we know if discrimination is occurring and then seek to eradicate it.

The staff who had been involved in the original staff and curriculum development programme took a particular view of the involvement of senior management. This view could best be summarized as cynical, with the strong suggestion that senior management lacked a real commitment to this work and had been, as it were, shamed into it. In addition, the staff had predicted the resource and database problems that senior management raised and felt that this particular type of staff development work was unlikely to be embedded into institutional structures. In this sense, staff and curriculum development was project funded and project focused and was, therefore, likely to be marginal.

An important issue is resistance to staff and curriculum development work of this kind. Whether it is considered voluntary or compulsory, there will always be staff who will resist it; ethnic diversity is a highly politicized issue, but no more so than other aspects of discrimination. As suggested in FEU work (1989), there are common strategies of resistance. For example, when curriculum change is discussed it is common to have a response on the following lines: 'Don't you think we are bending over backwards for them?' or 'We treat everybody the same, we don't discriminate against anyone' or 'Don't you think curriculum change is unfair on *our* students?' Such resistance is common but needs to be tackled; the following are some possible answers.

- Yes, certainly. Aren't we bending over backwards to meet the needs of all our students?
- Who do you mean by *our* students?
- Since 50 per cent of black people in this area are unemployed compared with 10 per cent in the population at large, we probably *should* bend over backwards.
- Aren't they all our students? (FEU, 1989: 137)

Another way of looking at responses to resistance is in terms of a variety of strategies. As FEU (1989: 139) indicates, you could respond to resistance in a number of ways. First, statistics could be quoted on the success of black students in schools, so that their lack of access to HE becomes a paradox. Second, appeals to professionalism could be made, which would stress the entitlement that all students have to fair and equitable treatment. Third, there could be a discussion of good practice in other institutions, particularly where such good practice had allowed those institutions to expand recruitment. Fourth, the law could be referred to, particularly where resistance is most obdurate. A final example would involve acknowledging an objection to, for example, curriculum innovation and then offering a wider context; for example, that students aware of diversity in the curriculum will find that knowledge marketable when they seek employment. All the above at least provide a basis for dealing with resistance, although there is, of course, no guarantee that these often rationalistic responses will be effective. This does not mean that resistance will vanish or that people will cease to discriminate; in part, this is because discrimination is a matter not only of logical arguments and evidence, but of strongly held beliefs which have a powerful emotional significance and which are often supported by elements of structural discrimination.

Much of the resistance identified above might be termed strategic in that it is rooted in long-standing and accepted ways of doing things which have remained unchallenged, in part, because in HEIs there is rarely a strong constituency of black people to lobby for change. This can be contrasted with radical resistance, which includes a complete unwillingness to recognize that there is an issue at all. Put another way, there are always likely to be staff and students who oppose any attempt to deal with systems and behaviours that are discriminatory. It seems clear that policy can have a limited effect here, in that equal opportunities policies and policies against racial harassment are only likely to change behaviour and leave attitudes relatively untouched. In addition, any change is only likely to be effective in the more formal situations, such as lecture rooms. There are common complaints by black students in both HE and schools that discrimination is, as much as anywhere, experienced outside the formal learning environment, in refectories, in toilets, through graffiti. There are similar limitations to linking staff appraisal, which is now commonplace in HE, to equality issues of this kind, in that it is by no means certain that appraisal could or should be used to induce tolerance.

Again, we can indicate *aims* and *good practice*, give some *warnings* and identify *monitoring of outcomes*.

Aims
- The development of a non-discriminatory ethos in HE, with associated practice.
- The development of curricula responsive to ethnic diversity.
- The provision of a quality experience for black students.

Good practice
- Organize sessions well in advance of the expected date and get the support of key players in HE (heads of department, deans, academic registrars).
- Involve black trainers with expertise.
- Make the sessions workshop-based and use, as far as possible, practical examples from good practice in other institutions.
- Identify clear aims and outcomes for each session.
- Encourage participants to identify action plans for the short and long terms.
- Provide good servicing for the sessions: rooms, catering, access to photo-copying and so on.
- Initially, and perhaps always, make attendance voluntary.
- Emphasize both staff *and* curriculum development issues.

Warnings
- Remember that, for white staff, the issues are often sensitive and involve dealing with often entrenched and deep-seated ignorance and misunder-standing.
- Remember that there is considerable individual resistance and institu-tional inertia towards issues of equity.
- Be aware that resource issues will often be used to resist innovation and develop ways to respond.
- Be aware that much of the discrimination faced by black students occurs in their interactions with white students.

Monitoring outcomes
- Establish systems to monitor students' complaints regarding discriminat-ory practices by staff and students.
- Establish regular equal opportunities audits of institution/faculty.

Theoretical and conceptual implications

Staff and curriculum development strategies raise two important theoretical and conceptual issues: the debate about multiculturalism and anti-racism as this relates to higher education; and the debate about how we tackle preju-diced and discriminatory attitudes and behaviour.

Multiculturalism, anti-racism and higher education

We can distinguish between multiculturalism and anti-racism in the following way: the former is about learning about other people's cultures and the latter is about learning how minorities are excluded from opportunities and face discrimination. As suggested in Chapter 3, there were major limitations to multiculturalism in schools and there was considerable opposition to anti-racist education; in addition, much policy towards diversity in education has been, as Gillborn (1995) and others (e.g. Troyna and Carrington, 1990) suggest, deracialized. In other words, issues of race have been rendered insignificant in current debate, have been ridiculed and demonized – as in popular discussions of political correctness and positive action strategies – or have been seen as only technical issues that require technical, rather than practical political, solutions.

One of the themes of this whole book is that these issues are largely absent from HE and there has been no comparable development of policy towards diversity. In part, this is due to the emphasis on access and the underplaying of progression issues; in part, it follows from the narrow view of the curriculum identified above; finally, it relates to the idea that HEIs do not discriminate and that curricula are sacrosanct (see Chapters 1, 4 and 6).

As indicated above, there is a major divide between what FE colleges have done about issues of diversity and what HEIs have accomplished. In consequence of these and other factors, considerably more has been done in FE and a great deal of developmental material has been produced for the FE market. FEU (1989) is a particularly good example here, in that it does provide an approach to ethnic diversity which emphasizes both culture and structure and is, in consequence, anti-racist in tone and intent. In addition, as shown above, it works with a wide and sophisticated notion of the curriculum. There is no comparable project which has dealt with these issues in an HE context.

Dealing with prejudice and discrimination

It is as dangerous to *assume* that there is prejudice and discrimination as to reject their existence outright. What, then, would constitute empirical evidence that there is prejudice and discrimination? What would allow us to say who discriminates? Is there evidence that only a minority is prejudiced? According to the yearly *British Social Attitudes* (Jowell and Witherspoon, annually), there is widespread evidence of both prejudice and racism and little evidence that these are restricted to some social groups rather than to others. Therefore, explanations which seek to reduce the susceptibility to prejudice and racism to a minority, or to the possession of power or to the lack of it, seem to be ill-founded. Prejudice is ubiquitous and seems to remain so.

There are, however, two issues about prejudice and racism which arise from sociological studies, one about the understanding which people have about where it occurs and the other to do with how people talk when they are being prejudiced. Both of these have to do with the rhetoric of prejudice. National and local studies (Jowell and Witherspoon, annually; Baxter and Glasner, 1986), indicate that people recognize widespread prejudice and discrimination against black people but argue that it is commonly done by *other* people. So, when people are asked questions of the kind 'Are you prejudiced against black people?', they generally say they are not. When the focus of the question shifts to 'are other people prejudiced?', the answer is much more likely to be in the affirmative. While these cannot both be empirically true, this does demonstrate something about these issues. In essence, people feel uncomfortable in recognizing their own prejudice but not in assigning it to others.

Billig's and van Dijk's work takes this a stage further, by looking at some of the rhetorical and linguistic devices through which people either deny prejudice and discrimination or render it justifiable. Van Dijk (1993), in a study which includes discussion of corporate, managerial discourses on black people, indicates that race issues are treated with a mixture of ignorance, evasion and denial. When asked, managers will often not know, for example, how many black people they employ. In addition, they will often not use terms like race and minority ethnic group but will talk about nationalities and claim to have international employees (van Dijk, 1993: 131–4). When issues of positive action arise, there is regular hostility to employing what are frequently called aliens, and issues of quality come to the forefront. Positive action strategies are, for managers, equated with lowering quality. All of this coheres into an inconsistent set of views: a desire to be seen as tolerant and open-minded, a view of positive action as interference and a threat to quality, and a view that employees from minorities may be difficult. All this is structured around an opposition between the world of business, which is about technical issues, and the world of politics, which is where issues like fair treatment are rightly dealt with.

Billig *et al.* (1988) take a further step in analysing what we might call prejudice talk, and help us to understand why there is little self-defined prejudice but a lot of it as far as views of others are concerned. Simply put, people use language to deny prejudice in themselves but allow it to exist in others. This can best be illustrated by a common device: 'I am not prejudiced/racist but . . .' The *but* can have a whole range of meanings, which include: the idea that others are prejudiced; the view that reasonable people like me are not prejudiced but there is a minority of extreme people who are; the idea that black people are really a problem and therefore I am not prejudiced because real prejudice is based upon falsity and ignorance. For Billig *et al.* what is at issue is a distinction between unreasonable prejudice (what others do) and reasonable prejudice (what we do). Reasonable prejudice is interesting in that it involves people in a commitment to fairness and tolerance – which are after all what 'we' are committed to – in opposition to minorities who want special privileges which are unfair. This range of meanings suggests that prejudice and discrimination might be very widespread indeed even when we find that they are being consistently denied. It also draws attention to some major problems in tackling prejudice and racism, which are to do with the very slipperiness of the language itself.

The point of staff and curriculum development is to tackle issues of discrimination and racism in the full recognition that things are difficult to accomplish. We can contrast two approaches: the first has its origins in the optimism of Enlightenment thinkers, whose critique of prejudice was founded on the idea that it was based on error and could, therefore, be eradicated through providing people, who are perfectible and therefore wish to behave fairly, with the truth. The second involves a critique of Enlightenment optimism and argues that there is no necessary link between information and the absence of discrimination. In particular, in some of its manifestations, this view is profoundly pessimistic; for example, including the idea that people take pleasure in discrimination and hatred. Whichever of these views we take, and whether we believe they can be reconciled, there is the problem of how we deal with discrimination and set about making discrimination unacceptable in practice.

As Sivanandan (1985) indicates there is a wide variety of strategies for tackling discrimination, which include different types of race training. For him, the various forms of training are structured around two sets of opposed views: those views which emphasize the attitudinal bases of discrimination as against those which stress its structural bases; and those which emphasize the rational element in training as opposed to those which give greatest significance to affectivity. The lesson from Sivanandan's argument is that the least effective methods for training away prejudice and discrimination treat them as aspects of individual attitudes and see them as simply affective residues in otherwise rational people. Essentially, prejudice and discrimination are rooted in structures – the very structures in which the people being trained are embedded – and involve powerful emotional elements – hate, anxiety and aggression. This combination of structure and emotions is what makes effective training acutely difficult.

Useful texts

Additional material on multiculturalism and anti-racism and on tackling prejudice and discrimination can be found in James and Jeffcoate (1981), Sivanandan (1985), Sarup (1986), Gilroy (1987), Billig *et al.* (1988), Cohen and Rattansi (1991), Troyna (1993) and van Dijk (1993).

5

Black Support Groups in Higher Education

I just felt very visible and the first thing I noticed was I was the only black student in the group.

(Monica, Afro-Caribbean)

It is so easy to feel isolated in this place.

(Billy, Afro-Caribbean)

If there were a lot more black people in education [and] in my course I would feel a lot better . . . there is unity between black people and [so] you would not stand out.

(Spencer, Afro-Caribbean)

The idea, development and use of black support groups are likely to be central to dealing with the isolation of black students and their feelings that they are discriminated against, and providing a basis for action. It is important, however, to recognize that there are different experiences of isolation for different groups of black students: many black students in the traditional universities see social class differences as the roots of isolation; many Afro-Caribbean students, who tend to be older than other students, see these age differences as especially isolating; Asian women students – often studying locally – feel isolated from white women in HE and from their peers who are not in HE. In addition to these different experiences of isolation, it is clear that numbers of black students in a given course or department can be a crucial variable: where there are substantial numbers of such students – and this is often on more vocationally oriented courses – isolation is less acute, even where levels of discrimination are high. Where black students are in a minority, isolation is felt acutely. In the former case, there is also likely to be pressure for the formation and recognition of some system of black support groups.

The work in Bath and Bristol was able to evaluate an already existing black support group at City Polytechnic and also to support the development of a support group at City University. Both these cases were in departments which had substantial numbers of black students (20–30 per cent), and where students spent some of their time on placements, placements which, as it transpired, often yielded feelings of isolation and experiences of discrimination. The formation of a black support group had two main stimuli: concern among black students that they lacked a voice and lacked an input into not only the running of the department, but also the courses themselves; and concern among staff and students, concern that was not in fact derived from formal ethnic monitoring, that completion rates for black students were significantly worse than those for white students. These combined concerns saw the rapid development from an informal grouping, meeting whenever times and circumstance would allow, to a formally recognized support group with timetabled meetings and recognition on course management, departmental and course planning committees. This formalization also occurred against a background in which there were systems of student support – personal tutors, student counsellors – but systems which were not seen as relevant and appropriate by black students. In large measure this was because such systems were largely staffed by white people.

This formalization was not seen as unequivocally positive. Some black students were concerned that formalization would lead to incorporation and powerlessness. In other words they recognized the value of having a system which is controlled by black students and lacks an institutional location. This was, of course, exactly why many staff wanted a formalized structure; that is, one they could identify, pin down and deal with! Some white students felt that black students were getting extra recognition and representation within the departmental structures. In essence, they were failing to recognize the extent to which existing structures within faculties and departments were heavily dominated by white people. Finally, some staff were uneasy about the black students' role and influence, particularly on curriculum issues.

The evaluation of the support group was predominantly positive and this evaluation played a central role in the extension of support groups to City University. The starting point for the evaluation was a commonly held view that black students are located in what Barrington, an Afro-Caribbean student, called 'an oppressive racist education system'. The support group can therefore provide a number of things: support if things go wrong; a safe space to discuss black issues; a pressure group for, for example, curriculum change. These are indicated in the following: 'A support system for black students to talk freely and honestly and get advice from other students . . . a safe environment . . . a pressure group [providing] support and empowerment . . . developing and refining a black perspective [and] feeding that into courses . . . [it becomes] the only time we have black space' (Rose, Afro-Caribbean).

The desire for a safe space in institutions that have long histories of discrimination is commonly held by a wide range of groups – women, black people, the disabled, gay people – and is a call for a form of separatism. It is, however, a separatism which may only need to be temporary or spasmodic; that is, a response to circumstances. In the Bath and Bristol cases, black students required a support group which they themselves organized but which could also have effects on other institutional structures. This was a desire for support groups which were separate but influential; this uneasy balance is one of the reasons for the equivocal views of formalization discussed above.

The issue of placement was especially sensitive, for, as one student put it, summing up a general feeling: 'When I have done placements I am very conscious of the fact that I am Asian . . . it's fine on the course but when you go out to placements you sense it. You are sheltered at X [name of institution given] . . . I am aware of racism in the profession . . . and it will be different when I qualify and get into the real world' (Abtar, Asian).

Similar difficulties have been experienced by black students involved in teacher education when they spend time teaching in schools (see Showunmi and Constantine-Simms, 1995). The relatively cosseted nature of HE contrasts starkly with what happens on placements. It was particularly noticeable that attendance at support group meetings was at its height during placements, despite the difficulty of attending such meetings when placements did not support attendance. Students were fully aware that in HE they were relatively sheltered from the realities of employment, even though the HE environment was not one free from discrimination.

Issues of discrimination were especially obvious in the early stages of the development of the support group: 'We got a poor reaction from white students. They often feel threatened' (Dipak, Asian). That there was no real foundation for those feeling of threat shouldn't lead to them being ignored, but such feelings do point to the need for situations in which white students can address issues of race discrimination themselves. As indicated above in discussions of staff development for white staff, such developmental work cannot be restricted to staff, but must also be available to white students. There is clearly going to be contention over what, precisely, is available. As indicated in Chapter 4, there is a variety of ways of tackling racism, including anti-racist and race awareness training, and within this variety not all are equally effective (Sivanandan, 1985).

The strengths of department- or faculty-based support groups – which tend to include students on related courses – is that they can have influence on most of the things that directly affect students: curriculum, delivery, assessment and, it is hoped, resources. But it has to be recognized that such groups require significant numbers of black students to be effective and, as such, are difficult to establish in department or faculties where there are few, if any, black students. If student union societies do not, as many black students argued, provide the answer, then for black students in a small minority there need to be other strategies. These might include inter-department or inter-faculty groups, the provision of black mentors, from either within the HEI or outside, and the appointment of black counsellors. These last two are not, of course, necessary only where support groups are difficult to organize and maintain. Systems of mentoring and counselling may prove useful in all HEIs where there are black students.

The relationships between support groups and student union societies were equivocal. Some black students saw the ethnic identification of student union societies – Afro-Caribbean, Asian, Muslim and so on – as potentially or actually divisive. In addition, they felt that student union societies were, in the eyes of academics, of marginal significance and had little, if any, role to play in affecting the quality of the student experience. Student union activities were, for those academics, to do with leisure, sports and culture. Other black students saw such societies as essential in supporting students – in particular, in terms of minority ethnicities – and were well aware that the linking of societies to cultural identity could operate to divide black students from each other. The potential for division around ethnicity was not, however, a sufficient reason to oppose ethnically identified societies.

We can identify a number of significant stages in the development of black support groups. First, some *problem* will arise which impacts particularly on black students; for example, harassment or difficulties with progression. This will result in the establishment of a small support group which is issue-focused. This group exists primarily to develop space in which issues can be discussed and solutions explored. Second, *negotiation* occurs between the support group and the wider faculty or department. Frequently, this will produce suspicion on the part mainly of white staff that black students are asking for, and being granted, special help and assistance. Third, this process of negotiation will lead either to *trust* and *recognition* and the establishment of some firm footing for the support group, or to continued hostility and suspicion. Fourth, the support group will become a part of the normal workings of the department or faculty; it will, in that sense, be *routinized* and given access to resources, rooms, timetabled space and so on. Fifth, there may then develop concern among black students that the support group is being *incorporated* and rendered less powerful. These stages represent, in outline, the natural history of support groups.

This natural history is closely tied to many of the structural and behavioural features of higher education institutions themselves. The problems that stimulate the formation of support groups are often a result of a lack of monitoring or of staff development, together with a feeling among black students that, as a minority, they are not listened to. The difficulties in the phase of negotiation often result from unwillingness on the part of white staff to consider that there are distinct problems which black students face and distinct needs which they have. Trust and recognition are most likely to develop where there is openness on the part of white staff and this is most likely to be a precondition for the routinization of support groups. The fear of incorporation is likely to remain a constant possibility if we recognize that black students are usually in the minority and have not, generally, been centrally involved in arguing for their entitlements within higher education or in having their entitlements recognized and accepted.

We can again identify *aims* and *good practice*, give some *warnings* and suggest ways of *monitoring outcomes*.

Aims
• The development of systems of support which are student-led.

- Improvements in the quality of the student experience for black students.
- Enhancing progression through HE for black students.

Good practice
- Develop support groups which are student-led and in which students set the agenda.
- Integrate support groups into the workings of the faculty or department and provide faculty or department facilities if requested.
- Provide a means for the support group to feed findings/ideas into departmental or faculty committees and into course development.
- Emphasize voluntary membership and attendance at support groups.
- Where there is a placement element in courses, build attendance at support groups meeting into placements contracts.

Warnings
- Be aware that white students and white staff may find the idea of support groups for particular students unacceptable or threatening.
- Recognize that support groups may raise expectations that are difficult to meet.

Monitoring outcomes
- Monitor the frequency of racial incidents, in HE and during placements.

Theoretical and conceptual implications

Part of the debate about support groups relates to issues already discussed above, in particular the importance of cultural identity in providing a site of resistance to discrimination. However, there are deeper issues, including the distribution of power within institutions and how far the political movements of black people are distinct.

Power, resistance and new social movements

Following the work of Foucault (Gordon, 1980), there has been a rethinking and reconceptualization of the concept of power. Of particular importance for the study of race and education is the attempt to see power as more than a negative activity and, in so doing, to stress the related idea of resistance. Put most simply, power is not only about forbidding things but also about enjoining people to do things; this latter has the consequence of not looking like an exercise of power and also of foreclosing some alternative ways of acting. Every exercise of power, in addition, will involve some strategies of resistance, albeit ones that do not usually look like the more familiar forms of political activity associated with social class. As such, struggles around race, gender and sexuality are distinct and are very different from struggles around social class.

This reconceptualization of the idea of power relates to how distinct racial, and for that matter gender, politics are; that is, how far we can see both as examples of the politics of new social movements. Some time ago, Gilroy identified something distinct about black politics and has subsequently developed this into a fully fledged theory: 'Localised struggles over education, racist violence and police practices continually reveal how blacks have made use of notions of community to organize themselves' (Gilroy, 1981: 212). For Gilroy, black politics is distinct in two senses: first, it does not easily fit into the mould of class-based politics; second, there is a scepticism among black people about the relevance of such a class-based politics to their lives.

It is for this reason that Gilroy (1987) seeks to link an effective black politics to a theory of new social movements. In several ways what makes new social movements distinct politically is also what will make for an effective black politics. The links between new social movements and black politics include: an emphasis on non-negotiable demands which are non-instrumental; a role for direct action; a stress on the significance of group identity; a central place for the body; a strong religious and spiritual component; a localization in urban spaces; a focus on community and territoriality; a stress on resistance.

To an extent, black political movements in general and student support groups in particular are distinctive. In the case of support groups, there is a strong element of resistance, of community and territoriality (in particular, through the demand to have a voice and a space from which to use it), of non-negotiable demands and of an emphasis on identity. If we follow Foucault and recognize this distinctiveness, then the fear of incorporation may be exaggerated. If we accept that power comes from below, that it produces the conditions for the exercise of freedom and that the aim of power is not liberation but resistance, then the idea of incorporation is not on the agenda, for every attempt to incorporate will produce new opportunities for resistance. As Sandal (1986: 122) puts it, 'struggle and change always take place through co-optation, that, in fact, change is made possible by co-optation because, in the process of co-optation, in assimilating the resistance, the terms of power change.' Thus, in the case of support groups, their very entry into the structure of departmental and faculty structures changes how those structures operate, changes the configurations of power.

Power and institutions: institutional racism

If we face the situation in higher education that black students do face, then the seemingly irresistible power of institutional racism has to be recognized. While the reconceptualization of power discussed briefly above may take us away from the idea that institutions operate in this way, it is important to identify another, more insidious, direction from which the denial of institutional racism is coming. In the discourse of deracialization (Troyna, 1993; Gillborn, 1995), the root of the problem is not a racism which inheres in structures; rather, there is only individual prejudice and racism and those, themselves, are only minority things.

As Gillborn and Troyna suggest, educational policy and the politics of education have been deracialized in part through this denial that racism is either structural or common. This denial in itself leaves the solution to racism as one centred on changing attitudes, and casts those black people who say that they face racial discrimination regularly on a day-to-day basis as exaggerating or as being politically motivated. For sociologists it is important to challenge this denial of institutional racism and, in the case of education, this is not an altogether difficult thing to do. First, at the theoretical level, we would have to stress that institutions and the ways they operate are not just made up of the sum total of the actions of the individuals working in them. As such, it is possible to have non-racist individuals operating within racist institutions. Second, we would emphasize a number of studies which suggest that the denial of institutional racism is specious. Mortimore *et al.* (1988) argue that black children are regularly entering schools that as a whole are the most ineffective and the least likely to improve children's performance. Wright's (1987) study of examination setting indicates that black students are allocated exam sets that are below their measured abilities, with the outcome that equally qualified white students are advantaged. Tizard *et al.* (1988) show that, on entry to primary school, black and white children start from a position of equality. These three examples make it difficult to explain inequity in schools simply as arising from individual acts of racism by a minority of teachers. To do so locates the problem in individual acts of discrimination, ignores the wider context of racism outside schools, makes the behaviour of a minority of racist teachers more influential than the non-racism of the majority and makes it seem that prejudice exists in a vacuum separate from institutions and structures. It is as unconvincing to deny structural issues in the reproduction of racial discrimination in education as it would be to make a similar denial of such factors in how employers recruit black staff (see Chapter 7). In addition, as argued throughout this work, higher education is unlikely to be a special case in which discrimination is absent, and therefore there can be little comfort for staff in higher education in arguing that most of the hard evidence of discrimination is provided by schools and colleges.

Useful texts

Additional material on the debates about cultures as sites of resistance and on new social movements can be found in Gilroy (1987, 1993), Melucci (1989), A. Scott (1990), Matheu (1995) and Solomos and Back (1995).

Part 3

Monitoring and Progression

The major theme of Part 3 is the importance of issues of progression for black students. In essence, for them access is important, but only to the extent that they have access to an environment which delivers a quality experience and from which they can move successfully into employment. Therefore, it is important that monitoring in universities includes the monitoring of the experience of black students and of their success or otherwise when they leave university. Such monitoring of student experience and of progression into the labour market can then become important performance indicators for HE.

6

Ethnic Monitoring in Higher Education

While the Commission for Racial Equality recommends ethnic monitoring to employers (CRE, 1980), and large numbers of local authorities have set up systems of equal opportunities monitoring (Williams *et al.*, 1989), equal opportunities monitoring in general and ethnic monitoring in particular are not the rule in HE (Bird *et al.*, 1992b). This may seem surprising for two related reasons: first, funders, auditors and quality assessors are rightly concerned with progression and with the quality of the student experience; second, without monitoring it will be very difficult to identify whether some groups are performing less well than others and whether this is occurring because of structures of discrimination, structures which might, in effect, be operating in an indirectly discriminatory fashion (see Chapter 1 above).

Where systems of ethnic monitoring do exist in higher education they often do so alongside more general equal opportunities monitoring. Although the depth and thoroughness of monitoring varies across institutions, there is a general awareness that it is an essential aspect of the monitoring of the quality of the student experience and that assumptions cannot be made that all the diverse groups entering higher education institutions are receiving education of the same quality (Bird *et al.*, 1992b).

Ethnic enumeration and ethnic monitoring

> A distinction [must be] drawn between 'ethnic enumeration', the 'relatively' simple counting of student enrolments by ethnic origin and the presentation of these statistics by such variables as age, sex, faculty . . . and 'ethnic monitoring': the comprehensive scrutiny of all aspects of course marketing, applications, admissions, delivery and outcomes using both quantitative and qualitative measures.
>
> (Billingham, 1988: 4)

The issue is, in fact, not just a combination of quantitative and qualitative measures, but the issue of quality itself: 'we have been trying to move the debate to monitoring as a much wider process which will include . . . measures of quality' (HE manager, in Bird *et al.*, 1992b: 13). The rationale for monitoring therefore covers the whole experience of higher education for the student – what we might call the learning environment. This means that both simple counting of students and any analysis which looks only at entry to and exit from university or college are inadequate. However, even comprehensive monitoring is not an end in itself. Institutions need to be clear what they are going to use data for, to ensure that there are sufficient resources to carry monitoring out and to recognize that, of itself, monitoring does nothing: 'ethnic monitoring is not a panacea to improve access to higher education for black people, nor is it a panacea to guarantee the [quality of] the black student's experience . . . what [monitoring] can do is inform discussions of what ought to be done' (Bird *et al.*, 1992b: 17).

Attitudes to monitoring

There is remarkably little material dealing with attitudes in higher education to ethnic monitoring in particular, and equal opportunities monitoring in general. A questionnaire-based study of 140 admissions tutors in HE nationally indicates some of the attitudes towards monitoring and some of the resistance to it (Bird *et al.*, 1992b). There is a clear split between those who see monitoring as an essential basis for assessing the quality of the student experience and those who see is as a diversion. This is clear in the following two pairs of quotations: 'it can inform both the content and techniques of teaching and enable us to critically assess our practices', and 'it can help us to meet [the] goals and targets of our equal opportunities policy, monitor change and the lack of it . . . and spread ideas and good practice'. 'The origin of students – ethnic or otherwise – is of absolutely no relevance to the intake. All that matters is academic standards', and 'we do not wish to divert useful staff teaching time to the exercise' (all from Bird *et al.*, 1992b: 19–20).

These are irreconcilable views. On the one hand, monitoring is seen as central to any desire to open up access and improve teaching; on the other, it is seen as too costly and as bringing non-academic judgements into the selection process. Each of these positions has its problems: the more favourable view seems to come close to the panacea view that monitoring is a major solution, perhaps *the* solution; the unfavourable view at least implies that monitoring is an extra that can be added on should resources allow. In addition, it makes a far from verifiable claim that universities only use academic judgements when they select students. Those in favour of monitoring would argue that it is precisely one of its aims to show whether non-academic matters are involved in the process of selection.

The point at issue, then, is to steer a course between the sometimes naive optimism of those who see monitoring as the solution to all problems and those who oppose it as wasteful and an interference in the judgements of academics. Steering this course is difficult because we are dealing with entrenched positions. Indeed, admissions tutors who opposed monitoring also opposed other aspects of university provision to widen access and enhance progression; for example, admissions policies which target under-represented groups and curriculum innovations which respond to the diversity of students. In respect of admission policies, typical responses include 'none apply' and 'our admissions policy and practice include an equal welcome to all candidates with no racial or political bias' (Bird *et al.*, 1992b: 22–3); with reference to the curriculum, the views discussed in Chapter 1, that programmes in HE are neutral as far as ethnicity is concerned, are typical. However, resistance to ethnic monitoring in particular, and to equal opportunities policies and practices in general, go deeper than this. Having considered the sensitivities involved in setting up systems of monitoring and responded to these by careful preparation and staff development, one senior academic in a university recalled the following experiences:

> I had loads of letters . . . and people phoning me up saying I was racist asking these questions . . . there was one particular faculty didn't bother to do as I had asked [and show a film about ethnic monitoring] and it was from that faculty I had lecturers phone me saying 'why the hell are you asking students to do this, this is really racist, how could you possibly be doing this?' . . . what I got back was forms with 'I am from the planet Mars' . . . lecturers had [said] to students 'yes, you can put any old thing', so it was a mockery.
>
> (HE manager, unpublished transcript)

The central issue here is the assumption of the need for care when one is setting up systems of monitoring and how, even when care has been exercised, there is still considerable hostility. We might question this need for care without denying the importance of preparation for monitoring. There is, in fact, no case for special care when one is dealing with issues of ethnic diversity, for all students have an entitlement to fair treatment. In addition, there is rarely a commensurate concern with care and guardedness when, for example, systems for monitoring academic standards are being discussed. Part of the reason for this difference is that concern with academic standards is written into the systems of governance of HEIs, while concern with equity seems not to be so written.

Three accounts of this resistance are identified below which indicate the importance of both the self-perceived liberalism of many in HE and the new structural context of higher education.

> HE institutions have been hiding behind this popular veneer that they are liberal, democratic institutions and that anybody can come here, but looking at their admissions policy and their selection and recruitment procedures, and the way their course content and delivery is organized, it is no wonder you are not getting people from ethnic populations . . . particularly if they have been victims of formal institutional discrimination . . . in schools.
>
> (HE staff, unpublished transcript)

The first lesson is that the liberalism of HEIs is, as argued above on several occasions, profoundly rhetorical and may not, from the point of view of many black students, have a real foundation.

> I think this business of polys seeing themselves as universities [which are] independent is actually detrimental to equal opportunities policy because under LEAs you were subject to some pressures and you served · that community and the community [often] happened to be a minority community.

(HE staff, unpublished transcript)

The second lesson is that some HEIs have committed themselves to establishing national and international reputations for teaching and research, and this often has the effect of leaving them less concerned with their local, black communities.

> We are back to a stage where the polytechnic is not being accountable to the local community ... there are companies in Britain now who have good practice in equal opportunities ... vice chancellors and principals have as much power or more than company directors and are, in many ways, less accountable.

(LEA staff, unpublished transcript)

The third lesson is that the corporate status of HEIs has left many HEIs lagging behind many large employers in developing equal opportunities policies and practices, particularly as these can impact on students, and in seeking to serve clients who are seen as customers.

The paradox of many of the objections to monitoring is that they can be nothing other than common-sense opinion in the absence of monitoring itself. What the objections seem to reveal is a deep distrust of what is being seen as interference in neutral processes – admissions to HE and success within it. Many of the rejections of monitoring and the ideas that treatment is always, magically, equal resemble the justifications of prejudice identified in Chapter 4. This is the point behind views which see HE staff as not exhibiting discriminatory behaviour and define the problems which black students have as located in their cultures and backgrounds. The point, however, is that monitoring is a precondition for testing such tacit knowledge, as suggested in the following: institutions 'will be able to review provision and service delivery in the light of analysis of ethnic background information on their student body ... information will provide invaluable assistance in tackling specific issues ... [and] encourage compli[ance] with equal opportunities policies' (Sammons and Newbury, 1989).

Not only is monitoring a precondition for challenging tacit assumptions about what happens to black students in the entry game to HE and on their HE courses, but it will also clarify some of the tacit assumptions about fairness in the selection process and how far judgements about students are based solely on academic criteria. As we have argued elsewhere in this volume, a great deal of the process of selection of students (for example, the use of references from teachers and employers, the provision of information on hobbies and other interests) may involve non-academic criteria. While qualifications may indicate the suitability of students, information on hobbies and other interests can decide if students are acceptable, where acceptability is usually unrelated to ability to benefit from HE (see Jenkins, 1986, 1992; and Chapter 7 below). As such, details of interest and hobbies have a questionable role to play in the process of selection. Taking this argument further, qualifications as measures of suitability are themselves of questionable status, evidenced by HEIs' willingness to rely on the crudities of GCE A level scores and unwillingness to specify what they want from a potential graduate and to be clear about what indicates ability to benefit from higher education.

Setting up an ethnic monitoring system

> Always work with your student union. If you can convince the student union it is a good thing you are three-quarters of the way there . . . and work with your staff, so before you even start your staff and student body believe in it.
>
> (HE manager, unpublished transcript)

As suggested earlier, establishing a system of ethnic monitoring, especially one which is to do with more than a simple counting of students at entry and exit from courses, is a sensitive issue. The support of staff and students is clearly a precondition for success, and this support will require development work with staff and students. This, in itself, will be resource demanding. However, given development work with staff and students and adequate funding, there are three issues which can still, if ignored, limit the possibility of establishing an effective monitoring system. These are clarity over the rationales for monitoring, over how data are to be collected and analysed and over how those data are to be used.

Rationales for monitoring

The rationale for ethnic monitoring is, at one level, obvious. It is the only way that universities and colleges will be able to tell whether they are treating students equitably and whether they are recognizing the diversity of the students they recruit. Any self-congratulatory idea that institutions do treat all students equally can only be treated seriously if monitoring is in place. Monitoring therefore becomes one way in which institutions can assess the quality of the student experience and, therefore, a way in which the cosy rhetoric of accessibility can be seen to be more than simple rhetoric and have real meaning for black students.

Clear rationales are also important tactically. Without a clear rationale, even one with which some staff will disagree, it is unlikely that a system of monitoring will receive support. In other words, a lack of a clear focus in monitoring strategies will provide reasons why monitoring should not occur. Put positively, clear reasons will make it more difficult to sustain the sorts of opposition to monitoring indicated in some of the views discussed earlier. Although there is a danger that the rationales may be somewhat vague, indeed as vague as commitments to accessibility at institutional level, clear recognition of the importance which institutions attach to equity, fairness, trust and openness *are* important, if only as a basis for challenging the reality of those commitments.

Ethnic categories, form filling and data collection

Quantitative monitoring – for example, of numbers of students, the programmes they access, their qualifications on entry, their post-course destinations – has proved relatively straightforward for those institutions that have tried to do it. Computer systems, such as ISIS and IRIS, should further facilitate such monitoring. There are, however, two sets of related difficulties in quantitative monitoring: those associated with the design of monitoring forms and those associated with non-response rates. What is most important in the design of forms is recognizing that ethnic categories are far from neutral and carry a heavy set of political overtones, and that some of the reasons why students do not fill in forms is to do with a combination of not knowing what the form is for and not being familiar and/or happy with the categories used.

Most universities and colleges monitor ethnicity when students register for courses and use classifications of ethnicity that are based upon that used by the Office of Population Censuses and Surveys (OPCS):

White
Afro-Caribbean
African Asian
Indian
Pakistani
Bangladeshi
Chinese
Other/mixed
Not stated

Classifications may also include black Caribbean, black African, black – other, other – Asian. There is a clear rationale for this, in that comparison between institutions is possible only where there is the use of similar sets of ethnic categories. However, classifications derived from the OPCS categories limit the possibility of self-definition and use categories that are resonant with the history of colonialism. In part, non-response rates relate to both these design features of monitoring forms. Black students very often do not relate to, or understand, the reference to 'Asian', 'African', 'Afro-Caribbean' and so on. This is clear, for example, when students of dual heritage discuss monitoring forms: 'I didn't know which box to tick . . . in the end I ticked both the white and the black box' (Maria) and 'I am British and black . . . I don't know why I am being asked if I am Afro-Caribbean'(Delroy).

This view suggests a whole complex of issues: what it is to be black, what it is to be British, how receptive form filling is to self-definitions of ethnicity, what we mean by ethnicity in the first place. This complex of issues is often not addressed in the monitoring process and begins to explain the often large numbers of students – as many as 50 per cent – who do not fill in monitoring forms when they enter higher education, even though they are much more likely to have filled in the monitoring section of the Universities and Colleges Admissions Service (UCAS) application form. Non-completion relates, in part, to forms which are not user-friendly and are not administered in a supportive and sensitive way. Examples of bad practice in the design and use of forms are common: not explaining what the form is for or what will happen to it; including ethnicity questions alongside questions about date of entry to the UK; using 30 ethnic categories on a single form; inadequate briefing of those responsible for administering the forms (Bird *et al.*, 1992b). The dilemma of non-response rates which are a result of poor forms and poor administration of them is, as we will see below, that the data that are produced will be inadequate and that inadequacy easily becomes a basis for not continuing with such monitoring and for opposing policy moves to address the problems which black students face.

There is a further point about ethnic classifications, and that is how they treat 'white' as a unitary and unproblematic category. This is a deeply rooted problem in the sense both that white includes a wide variety of ethnicities – Welsh, Scottish, Polish, English and so on – and that this category presents white people as having something in common. In this sense, the category 'white' is empty in a way that minority ethnicities are not. Minority ethnicities, with all their history rooted in colonialism, form the basis on which data is collected, data which fundamentally construct monitoring around racial divisions.

There is, finally, a series of practical issues concerning the administration of ethnic monitoring forms. Across HEIs there is a variety of systems; in some the ethnic section is included in the enrolment form, while in others it is a separate form. The former, in indicating the importance of the exercise, seems to be more effective in producing high response rates and these rates are highest where a clear, explanatory letter is provided. This letter needs to include the reasons for monitoring, explain the ethnic categories which are being used and the uses of ethnic data, and is most effective where it is signed by a senior member of the institution. Whoever is responsible for overseeing the enrolment exercise needs to be made fully cognizant of the importance of monitoring and be able to explain the process to students. As suggested earlier, a lack of commitment from staff will severely affect both response rates and the quality of information. Good practice includes:

the use of a letter from senior management giving their full support to the ethnic monitoring exercise which [goes] to all students and staff; the inclusion of [the] ethnic monitoring question in a section which also asks about gender and special needs; the placing of the ethnic monitoring question[s] towards the beginning of enrolment forms; making the ethnic monitoring statistics available to students.

(Bird *et al.*, 1992b: 39)

When those involved in the monitoring process – either central staff or those in faculties and departments – treat the exercise cynically, data will be incomplete and provide little basis for policy decisions and changes. There is no doubt from the above that there is some cynicism which can manifest itself in both covert and overt opposition and resistance.

The uses of ethnic data

The lowest responses [to ethnic monitoring forms] were from BEd courses which have a high percentage of black students.

(HE staff, unpublished transcript)

Less than half the students responded, that doesn't give a very powerful lever ... at the moment the information is not sufficiently well formed in the case of ethnic origin ... to address the [issue] of drop out.

(HE staff, unpublished transcript)

In many HEIs, the response rate to ethnic monitoring forms is low. White students often do not answer because the exercise is seen as of no interest to them and, as indicated above, may be taken less than seriously by white staff. Black students often do not respond because, as Bhat *et al.* (1988) suggest, they are suspicious about whether the data will become the basis for policy changes and, if so, whether those changes will work to their benefit. Finally, senior managers see non-response as a failure in the whole exercise and are therefore inclined to reject any policy changes based upon partial data.

For white staff and students the lack of positive attitudes to monitoring and to form filling is, as suggested above, part of their overall resistance to the process and to what they see as the outcome of the process: 'what I would not be happy to do is to exercise any discrimination on the basis of special pleading for single-issue pressure groups' (HE staff, unpublished transcript). Again the understanding of outcomes is, at best, muddled and frequently centres on fears about interference in already fair procedures, particularly in reference to admissions and to the curriculum: 'it is other people's responsibility if there are not enough people [with] A levels to join courses ... the work we do is colour-blind' (HE staff, unpublished transcript). 'I would be immediately open to attack if I attempted to introduce a Muslim dimension into the teaching of engineering . . . I would be open to attack from Jews, Hindus, Christians and all' (HE staff, unpublished transcript). For black students there is scepticism about whether anything will happen as a result of monitoring and whether any changes will be to their benefit.

Finally, outcomes of ethnic monitoring are dependent upon comprehensive data. The lack of such data is both a genuine reason for failing to take action – after all, action does require some underpinning of accurate, statistical data – and an excuse where there is no real commitment to action in the first place: 'Until we can produce the data to tell other people in the institution, especially senior management, that there is a problem here it is going to make it very hard to deal with these issues' (HE manager, unpublished transcript).

Equality policies and equality audits

There is danger in only monitoring ethnicity: 'I think the trouble at the moment is, because you don't have general statistics, it is exactly when ethnic minority students run into difficulties that you become aware of ethnic minority students. You forget to take account of the successful [ethnic minority] students who go through without problems' (HE staff, unpublished transcript).

There are two lessons here. First, as far as ethnic monitoring is concerned, monitor all black students, as otherwise a system which is designed to identify structural problems will easily become one which stigmatizes those black students who, for whatever reason, are in difficulties. One essential point is that monitoring is as likely to indicate good practice by institutions and success by students as structural and individual failure. Another is that there is an uneasy relationship between the identification of students who are in difficulties and how white staff deal with such students. Again, there is a commonly held view that there is a limit to what staff can do, and this is set by the culture, history and background of black students: 'If, within a community it is the culture for women not to be educated, then there is very little we can do about it' (HE staff, unpublished transcript). 'There is the case [of] an Asian student who has immense cultural difficulties, her parents are not in sympathy with her wanting to be a teacher, she has to rely on her own finances. We sympathize but, in the end . . . we can only help so far' (HE staff, unpublished transcript). 'My own experience has been, when we look at ethnic minorities . . . Asian students often actually tend to achieve beyond their potential, whereas Afro-Caribbean students do not . . . it's actually the cultural position of the person's parents and how long they have been in Britain' (HE staff, unpublished transcript). Here we see the general unwillingness to consider that structural issues are at the heart of the problems faced by black students and to indulge in culture-blaming.

Second, monitor all students regardless of their ethnic and/or minority status. There is an obvious reason for this and this is that differential performance and differential educational experiences are common to all groups of students. As Farish *et al.* (1995: particularly Chapter 8) argue, there is a need for a coherent and cohesive set of equal opportunities policies and related practices, with a linked and coherent support structure. The dangers lie both in only monitoring ethnicity and in having a series of fragmented policy initiatives without any overall framework of support.

Finally, there is the issue of auditing in respect of ethnic and other forms of monitoring. One of the major themes of much of the work carried out by the FEU (especially 1987a, b, 1989), is that issues of equity affect everything that happens in institutions. They are not something that is only to do, for example, with completion of degrees or with how we admit students. This suggests that monitoring will need to be part of a more general equality audit of institutional provision. As argued above (Chapter 4), there will not be a quality service if aspects of that service are covertly or overtly discriminating against students. The lessons learned in schools, where there has been recognition of problems such as name calling in the playground, must be learned by HEIs. The essential lesson is that discrimination *is* widespread. There is every possibility that liberal education institutions will still contain areas of discrimination. Auditing is a precondition for knowing whether this is happening, and this is probably why the then Polytechnics and Colleges Funding Council took such a strong line on monitoring: 'It is clear, however, that the achievement of a closer relationship between policy objectives and policy outcomes, at both sector and institutional levels, requires a greater emphasis on setting targets and monitoring progress' (PCFC, 1992: 24).

What, then, would an ethnicity audit include? At the simplest level, such an audit would assess all services in terms of how they recognize, and respond to, ethnic diversity. As suggested above, this will include academic and non-academic services. There will be a central concern with both policy – for example, over curriculum issues, recruitment targets, harassment – and how these policies work over periods of time. This form of auditing would not, in practice, be any different from that which occurs within institutions and is done, externally, by the Higher Education Quality Council (HEQC). In that sense, the aim would be for it to become a part of the normal operations of HEIs. Of course, moving towards a situation where it does become routine may be difficult, if for no other reason than that HEIs have rarely taken issues of ethnic diversity seriously and because the surrounding social climate is one in which such issues are often ridiculed. One possible claim could be that such auditing is a form of political correctness. One possible response to this is that, in fact, we should be politically correct in recognizing and responding to diversity.

In summary, *aims*, *good practice* and some *warnings* are set out below.

Aims
• Providing a basis for a measure of the quality of the student experience.

- Providing a basis for a measure of progression.
- Providing a basis for responsiveness to client needs.

Good practice
- Establish comprehensive monitoring using quantitative and qualitative measures.
- Fund monitoring adequately and over a long time period.
- Embed monitoring throughout the organization.
- Establish staff development as a basis for setting up and maintaining systems of monitoring.

Warnings
- Expect resistance to comprehensive monitoring.
- Expect that existing hardware will not do the job you want.
- Expect comprehensive monitoring to be resource intensive.

Theoretical and conceptual issues

Three issues relating to ethnic monitoring are worthy of attention here: the uses to which knowledge of black people is, and can be, put, that is, the politics of knowledge; the merits of quantitative and qualitative measures and of their triangulation; the merits, or otherwise, of positive action strategies.

The uses of knowledge

Booth (1988), Ohri (1988) and Gordon (1992) emphasize that statistics on race and ethnicity are unlikely to be neutral in terms of either their collection or their interpretation. The first issue – their collection – has already been mentioned and one of the major difficulties alluded to; that is, the categories used to collect racial data. They contain a mixture of racial categories (for example, colour), of national categories (for example, Pakistani) and of ethnic categories (for example, Chinese). The last is, of course, both ethnic and national (Gordon, 1992: 20–1). This mixture is problematic in terms of how people fill in questionnaires. The use of the term black African on a monitoring form is doubly problematic, in that it uses the term black in a non-political sense (that is, black as implying oppression) and is pseudo-racial in that black is seen as descriptive. Moreover, African implies some kind of identity with an origin, just as Pakistani implies identity with a nation, even for people who are British citizens. This complexity doesn't make the filling in of forms or the interpretation of the statistics any the easier. Indeed, while it might be important for many purposes to know what people mean when they self-identify as black, this meaning cannot be derived from their answers.

If there are problems with categories and interpreting race/ethnic statistics, there is also little consensus about why the data are being collected at all. As Gordon (1992: 25–34) indicates, there is a division between those who favour collection because it provides factual data which can inform policy and provide a basis for social reform, and those who oppose the collection on the grounds that data can and have been abused and that there is no agreed and agreeable set of definitions of what constitutes race and ethnicity on which to base the collection. As Ohri (1988) and Booth (1988) suggest, this divide of opinion is itself racial: white people are somewhat more likely to favour collection and black people to oppose it. For the sociologist there is a theoretical and an empirical issue here. The theoretical issue relates to the status of fact finding and an increasing scepticism about the idea of politically neutral facts which are just waiting to be identified. The empirical issue is whether racial data have had a positive effect, have led to major changes in policy. Scepticism is the rule here, as a quote from John Rex in Gordon (1992: 28) indicates: 'The benefit which immigrants have had from racial statistics has been confined largely to help on technical matters, like language instruction. Otherwise, the presence of immigrants has been used as an index of pathology, justifying increased payments to particular local authorities who have all too often used such increased payments for the benefit of their native British citizens.' Put another way, some legislation aimed at supporting ethnicity minorities has been based partly on data; for example, the 1976 Race Relations Act. However, there is much that is negative in policy terms which has been based upon ethnic data of various kinds; here, we might include the variety of immigration controls, the controversies about mugging as a black crime and concern about 'illegal' asylum seekers. All of these – seemingly derived from statistical data of impeccable pedigree – have served to pathologize large number of black people. In the end we must conclude that the statistical is political.

Quantitative and qualitative measures

Part of the debate about quantitative and qualitative methods relates to the debate about the scientificity or otherwise of the social sciences. It is a debate that has never been resolved and has produced, at best, a stand-off in which researchers try as far as possible to use methods that are appropriate to what they are doing and to use a variety of methods – what has been termed triangulation – in order to gain a number of perspectives on a given topic. There is, in fact, considerable debate about triangulation, debate which can be summarized in this quotation from Silverman (1993: 158):

> the major problem with triangulation as a test of validity is that, by counterposing different contexts, it ignores the context-bound and skilful character of social interaction and assumes that members are 'cultural dopes' who need a sociologist to dispel their illusions . . . a

better solution might be to distinguish 'how' from 'why' questions and to triangulate methods and data only at the 'why' stage.

The further danger in an emphasis on triangulation is that we underplay the advantages of particular methods for particular purposes. Thus, qualitative methods are appropriate in some circumstances but we must keep in mind their limitations. These limitations are well summarized by Silverman (1993: 196–211) in his six rules of qualitative research, which I slightly paraphrase in the following. First, do not mistake a critique of a method as a reasoned basis for the alternative. In other words, a critique of quantitative methods does not establish the case for the superiority of those that are qualitative. Second, avoid treating actors' points of view as explanations for what is being studied. This is difficult to achieve and has undoubtedly occurred in some of the above discussion. The point, however, is that interview data are not raw or true data but are situated and textual. Third, we must recognize that the phenomenon always escapes in the messy world of fieldwork. Fourth, always avoid choosing between polar opposites, such that the structural context of people's views is seen as more important than the meanings they give to their context. Fifth, never appeal to a single element as an explanation, but be prepared to recognize a multiplicity of elements. Finally, understand that truth is a constructed, cultural form.

Several of these issues have been acutely problematic in the work on racism on which much of the discussion in this book has been based. The phenomenon of racism rarely escaped; indeed, it often became the single factor for black students in HE and schools, with issues of class and gender taking second place. This contrasted interestingly with the total absence of issues of race from discourses of deracialization. In addition, it is difficult not to take the actors' views on the ubiquity of racism as an explanation; that is, as more than simply examples of racism.

There is also, for the researcher, an issue over which data are seen to be most powerful in the public domain, and there is little doubt that statistical data have a dominant position in the politics of knowledge.

In race research, as indicated above, both quantitative and qualitative data have to be viewed with care and sometimes with suspicion. If we can get over that difficulty, then there is considerable value in qualitative research in that what we are often interested in is the experiences of people which, as it were, lie behind the statistics on educational achievement. These experiences, as argued on a number of occasions above, are best derived from carefully carried out ethnographic studies, including interviews with both individuals and groups. Such studies do, of course, have their own unique problems, in particular the interpretation of qualitative data and how we move from the individual account to the larger picture. The advantage of triangulation is that it provides a basis for a combination of types of analysis and depth of analysis. Qualitative and quantitative studies can become mutually reinforcing and provide a combination of general trends and detailed biographies.

The relevance of positive action strategies

Positive action strategies have, predominantly, been developed in the context of employment and, where the concern is with ethnicity, have had four major stimuli: that ethnic minorities do not apply for employment; that they are not selected; that they are not promoted; and that they are not retained. These usually apply even when black applicants are well qualified and could do the jobs for which they are applying. These four provide the basis for positive action programmes and allow us to evaluate them: do such programmes increase black applications, selection, promotion and retention? All these can, with minor modification, be applied to the context of black students in HE: do they apply? Are they selected? Are they retained? What is the outcome of their studies?

As we have already seen, black students apply to HE and are admitted. Allowing for this, some groups do considerably less well than others – Afro-Caribbean men are probably least successful. If we take positive action to include strategies to increase applications *and* strategies to train people to become applicants and to succeed once admitted, two things are noticeable. First, there is a limited set of measures which HEIs take to increase applications from some groups of black people; indeed, many in HE see the lack of black applicants as not their problem. Second, there is also a limited set of measures to upskill those black people who have had negative experiences of school and college education. There is a third, related point, and that is that, because of the lack of ethnic monitoring, there is little data on progression by black students once they enter HE.

The majority of evaluations of positive action programmes have been in the industrial and business context, and with reference to encouraging people to apply for jobs and offering them training to improve their promotion opportunities. Welsh *et al.* (1994) and Jewson *et al.* (1995) indicate some of the likely problems in developing effective strategies and some of the conditions for success.

In terms of encouraging black people to apply for jobs, Welsh *et al.* (1994: 25–6) point to the importance of using existing networks to inform people of available opportunities and of using a variety of channels. The point is that there are existing networks (for example, within black communities) which might go unnoticed by employers. Equally important is dealing with black people's reservations about employment with an organization, in particular, where there has been no history of black employment or where black employees have had negative experiences. Finally, sustained contact with black people is crucial. One-off initiatives in black communities may raise the company profile but are unlikely to be successful and will probably increase levels of cynicism as to the intentions of employers. In terms of retraining programmes (Welsh *et al.*, 1994: 26–8), success is likely to come when there are available employment outlets post-training, such that trainees are likely to progress. In other words, training needs to be integrated into company recruitment procedures. In addition, the training needs to be relevant and appropriate, done by quality trainers and accredited and therefore portable. What works and does not work is fairly easy to identify. Difficulties occur when there is no top-level commitment to positive action, where positive action strategies have no clear objectives, where line managers are not involved, where employees are not consulted as to the issues involved and where monitoring is absent (Welsh *et al.*, 1994: 31–6). Successful strategies therefore require senior and line management commitment, clarity of objectives, systems to monitor the achievement of objectives, employee involvements and quality training. Finally, we can refer to the work of Jewson *et al.* (1995), where it is suggested that effective equal opportunities practice occurs when these practices are the outcome of real workplace issues, those affected by the policies are involved in their development and operation, and equal opportunities issues are seen as an integral part of policy and practice in general. This long list of criteria for the success of positive action strategy and equal opportunities policy is unlikely to need altering in the HE context. Indeed, many HEIs have such policies and practices for staff but have yet to consider how they might apply them to students. If, for example, an employer develops training schemes to encourage black applicants for employment as part of a positive action policy, there seems no reason why an HEI should not do something similar to encourage applicants from groups of black students who are not, as yet, ready to apply.

Despite the emphasis on what makes a successful policy in the work of Jewson *et al.*, Welsh *et al.* and others, it is as well to keep in mind Jenkins's (1992) work and the ubiquity and stubbornness of acceptability criteria and stereotyping (see Chapter 7 below). As we will see, even where black people are suitably qualified to enter employment, criteria of acceptability – appearance, manner, language and so on – seem to disadvantage them systematically in practice. As a preliminary to a consideration of access to employment in Chapter 7, we can quote from Gibbon, who presents a healthily sceptical view of policy for equality:

> To sum up these research findings, there appears to be little or no relation between possession of even a developed and implemented EOP [equal opportunities policy] ... and stimulating change in employment outcomes, at least in the short-term. Where the latter had occurred to the advantage of black people, this was driven by political decisions within organizations to prioritize the equalization of outcomes, often in conscious distinction to 'being fair to everybody'. The meaning of positive action for employers who took these decisions was not as a supplement to 'being fair to everybody', but as a set of techniques enabling organizations which had decided to employ disadvantaged groups in greater numbers to conform to the letter of the law. It is possible, furthermore, that the factors making for the adoption of decisions facilitating equality of outcome are antithetical. On the whole, EOP development seems plausibly linked to bureaucratization, and possibly appeals

to bureaucratic organizations . . . because of its formalizing qualities. Moreover, the more bureaucratic an organization is, the more it is arguably likely to pursue implementation seriously. The promotion of equality of outcome, by contrast, requires the suspension or sidelining of bureaucratic norms and procedures within an organization and (at least temporarily) the elevation of politics to a position of command.

(Gibbon, 1992: 248–9)

Useful texts

Additional material on the debates about the politics of racial data, on triangulation of methods and on the effectiveness of positive action can be found in Paul *et al* (1987), Bhat *et al.* (1988), Skellington and Morris (1992), Welsh *et al.* (1994) and Jewson *et al.* (1995).

7

Progression beyond Higher Education

If we accept that, regardless of fluctuations in employment markets, one of the central aims and outcomes of higher education is access to quality jobs, then the experience of black people exiting from universities and colleges is, to say the least, equivocal. Put another way, the window of opportunity opened by higher education is more open for some groups of black students than others. This can be indicated in a number of ways.

Qualifications and unemployment

Whereas, in the period 1988–90, 3 per cent of white people with degrees were unemployed, the figures for people of Pakistani, Chinese and African origin were 9, 5 and 8 per cent respectively; for all minorities, the figure was 6 per cent (Jones, 1993: 116 and 127). At this most basic level, therefore, the payoff of having an HE qualification is greater for white people than for many people from minority ethnic groups.

Qualifications and employment

There is evidence that well qualified black applicants for jobs face discrimination and that there is more discrimination against the well qualified black person than ones with fewer qualifications. In addition, if we take those with maximum qualifications as GCE A levels and GCSEs respectively, then for the former groups, Afro-Caribbean men do worse in employment than white men, and for the latter all ethnic minorities do worse than comparable white men (Hubbock and Carter, 1980; Clough and Drew, 1985; Ohri and Shaista, 1988; Jones, 1993: 71–2).

For graduates, the studies by Brennan and McGeevor (1987, 1990) and Brennan and Jarry (1991) are still the most comprehensive and indicate that 'although the immediate job prospects for black graduates appear to be less favourable than for their white peers, the black graduates perceive a greater range of more general benefits from higher education' (Brennan and McGeevor, 1987: 40). On the latter, the conclusion is interesting: 'While the perceived benefits for white graduates tended to be greater in terms of individualistic goals, for black graduates they were greater for aims with a more social orientation' (p. 38). The conclusions from Brennan and McGeevor generally support the picture discussed above. Black graduates have greater difficulty getting employment than comparable white graduates and they gain jobs inferior to those of their white counterparts. For Asian students this is particularly interesting, as they are more likely to do more broadly vocational degrees than other groups and might, therefore, be expected to have little difficulty in entering the labour market. As Brennan and McGeevor (1987: 72) conclude: 'there is a clear message for employers and careers advisers: that black graduates are receiving unequal treatment in the labour market and that action will be required to remove it.'

It is, therefore, clear that there is more to gaining employment than objective criteria such as qualifications, and that whatever these additional factors are, they bear heavily on some or all groups of black people. Some insight into processes of selection as these impact on black people is given in Jenkins's (1986, 1992) work. Jenkins makes an important distinction between criteria. Some are functionally specific to a job, and include qualifications, experience and ability to do the job. Black workers are as likely to meet these criteria as white workers. These criteria define whether someone is suitable for a job. Where these are lacking there is a specific role for positive action programmes, which can provide both pre-entry training to improve the chances of someone meeting these specifications and in-job training which improves the chances of advancement. However, there is a second set of criteria which are functionally non-specific and relate to acceptability for a job. In essence, you can be suitable but not acceptable.

For Jenkins, acceptability criteria are tacit, depend upon cultural competencies and, in consequence, will bear especially on black people. Acceptability criteria fall into three categories: primary, to do with appearance, manner, attitude and maturity; secondary, associated with gut feeling, speech, age, marital status, labour market history, literacy and the ability to fit in; and tertiary, linked to English language competence and a reference from a past employer. These are tacit in the sense that they rarely, with the possible exception of linguistic competence, form part of job descriptions and person specifications, and provide leeway for refusing people who are, formally, suitable. This leeway may be viewed as important by those appointing, in part because of opposition to rigidly specific formal criteria and a desire to have large degrees of discretion in the appointment process. Therefore, views on ability to fit in may exclude a person who is otherwise qualified to do a job.

However, these acceptability criteria are, for Jenkins, likely to have a disproportionate effect on black people. We can indicate this with an example from each category. Manner and attitude are especially problematic:

> considering the importance of non-verbal communication . . . a white
> recruiter may choose to interpret an avoidance of direct eye contact by

an applicant as indicating anything from a lack of confidence to 'shifti-ness'. However, for many job seekers whose cultural background lies in the Indian sub-continent, the refusal of eye contact may be a respectful attempt to avoid impoliteness. For many managers I interviewed such behaviour in an interview would be an indicator of unacceptability.

(Jenkins, 1992: 151)

We might add here that the issue is the manager's attitudes and precon-ceptions and not what is, in effect, the assumed pathology of the applicant's culture.

Gut feeling and ability to fit in as secondary criteria are more clearly prob-lematic, in that they assume a culture and ethos of an organization that may already have no black workers. In this case, ability to fit in and being black may be inimical to each other. However, there are also problems with seem-ingly more objective criteria like employment history. If, as seems to be the case (Jones, 1993: 71–2, 112–33), black workers are more likely to experience unemployment or to be employed at levels below what their qualifications would indicate, then relying on job history may adversely affect judgements of acceptability.

Finally, with reference to English language competence and references there can be difficulties. As Jenkins (1986: 68–9; 1992: 152) suggests, em-ployers may set standards of competency in English too high for jobs and, although they often test or rely on tests of literacy, they rarely assess com-petency with the same rigour. The reliance on references is also problem-atic if we concede that these are most likely to come from white employers, who can sometimes themselves discriminate in either covert or overt fashion.

The existence of acceptability criteria also, for Jenkins (1986: 82–95), interacts with stereotyping of minority ethnic groups. Stereotypes that are commonly held – Afro-Caribbean people are lazy/aggressive/unreliable – interact with and reinforce ideas about acceptability. Managers may, there-fore, use ideas that negative stereotypes of black people are widespread as a reason for not employing them. Acceptability criteria may often look as though they are formal, rational and an essential part of the appointment process which allow managers some discretion in whom they appoint. Ste-reotypes do not have that same aura of reasonableness.

It is clear that having a degree, GCE A levels or GCSEs is no guarantee of high-quality, high-status employment. We can, in fact, develop this argu-ment in two directions. The first would look at the often disadvantaged position of well qualified black people, including those who have been through higher education. The second would consider the types of jobs to which well qualified black people are more likely to gain access.

Schematically, we could argue that the exclusion of well qualified people from jobs and their over-qualification for the jobs they are doing is, itself, an effect of racism. To the extent that long-standing attitudes have cast black people as inferior and lacking in ability, well qualified black people are an especial paradox. Equally schematically, the concentration of black people in some high-status jobs – social work, for example – is, in part, to do with ideas about black communities servicing their own needs and those needs being most appropriately met by black people. In the language of a colonialism which is deeply influential on relationships between black and white people, we have a system of indirect rule.

What are the payoffs of HE?

As we have seen, Brennan and McGeevor (1987, 1990) argue that there is more to what people get out of study in universities and colleges than something which facilitates access to the labour market. While white students are instrumental in orientation, black students see wider social benefits to higher education, including becoming better educated to improve society, becoming more widely educated and improving social status.

There is a number of ways of understanding these different motivations. First, it is further evidence of the high value placed on education by black people (see Eggleston, 1993). It seems that this high value is associated with much more than employment and income. Second, it may say something about the political socialization of black and white people; that is, a socialization based upon strong cultural pressures for educational attainment among, for example, parents who did not benefit but who have a view on the value of education. However, part of these different motivations may involve a coping or survival strategy for those people who recognize that having a degree is no guarantee of success for those who live in a racist society.

8

Conclusions: A Policy for Equality

It is around issues of ethnic diversity that the liberal ethos of higher education institutions comes face-to-face with the evidence of discriminatory
attitudes and practices. These attitudes and practices commonly face black
students throughout their educational histories, and HEIs have lagged behind
both schools and FEIs in recognizing this and attempting to respond. It is
the case that black students are entering HE in increasing numbers, are
entering an increasingly wide range of programmes and are progressing
through HE and gaining qualifications. It is equally the case that many
of them accomplish this while being discriminated against and feeling
isolated. As such, there are problems with the quality of the black experience of HE, problems which are not fully recognized – especially given the
haphazard nature of ethnic monitoring – and which are often not being
tackled. When black students leave higher education, many of them face the
same problems of graduate unemployment as other graduates, but with the
additional disadvantage of the higher rates of unemployment facing many
black people generally, and the problems faced by well qualified black
people seeking quality employment.

This general picture disguises some differences between groups of black
students. For example, Afro-Caribbean men in HE under-perform compared with Afro-Caribbean women; Chinese students do particularly well
compared with other groups, both black and white. While we should not
underplay these differences, it is still the case that successful access and
successful exit from courses is not the end of the matter; on-course experience is important even if it does not appear adversely to affect performance. Indeed, the importance of on-course experience is indicated by the
nature of the funding councils' teaching quality assessment system; in this
system, judgements of quality are explicitly linked to what it is like to be a
student. As suggested above, the system may not go far enough in explicitly
addressing issues of *equality* assurance, but there is at least the potential for
identifying student diversity as an essential issue in the quality of teaching. This conclusion has three sections. First, attention is given to some of
the experiences of black students in universities and colleges in the USA.
Second, a threefold reformulation of concerns focusing on progression, the

learning environment and equality assurance is considered. Finally, some aspects of equality policy are explored.

Interlude: the American experience

There is, as might be expected, a considerable body of work on black students in the USA. Within that work, studies of black students in white institutions (for example, Sedlacek *et al.*, 1974; Sedlacek and Webster, 1978; Burrell, 1980; Astin, 1982; Taylor, 1986; Sedlacek, 1987) are of particular interest even when we recognize the differences between the American and British systems of higher education.

Sedlacek (1987) provides the most useful summary and develops a model for studying the black experience and for developing policy responses which has useful possibilities for black students in Britain. Success for black students is much more rooted in experience than it is related to ability; able black students will therefore fail to progress and/or will see the HE experience as traumatic and devaluing. The HE environment does not, therefore, fully accept them, in part because of a predominantly white ethos. In arguing this, Sedlacek identifies seven variables which make for success for black students and whose absence prefigures under-achievement. These variables are self-concept, self-appraisal, how racism is dealt with, previous experience of community service and of leadership, availability of support, access to non-traditional knowledge and the nature of goal setting.

Not all of these are applicable to the British context and there has, for example, been considerable discussion of ideas of self-esteem, particularly where this idea has been tied to a notion of low *black* self-esteem (see, for example, Stone, 1980). This critique of low self-esteem seeks to relate how black people see themselves to the foreclosure of many opportunities in education and employment, so that what may look like low self-esteem can be reconceptualized as having realistic expectations.

However, a number of Sedlacek's variables *are* of relevance. Realistic self-appraisal is important for all students, in particular because it provides a basis for not only how students work but also how they value themselves. The US experience suggests that white staff may either undervalue or overvalue black students and, in addition, that black students get the best bases for self-appraisal in black colleges and universities. Undervaluing students is obviously problematic, as it can lead staff to underestimate how well a student will perform in the future and may serve to affect real levels of performance. Overestimating a student's ability is also a problem, particularly at points of transition from one programme to another. If there is an unwillingness to inform black students accurately about how they are doing, especially if they are moving from one level of education to another, this can lead to great difficulties later in the educational system. The point is that there may be a strain of liberalism in white academics which makes it difficult for them to tell black students that they are doing less well than they might expect. Both underestimating and overestimating the ability and performance of black students serves, quite reasonably, to make them less trusting of white academics and institutions.

Strategies for dealing with racism and support systems, including black mentors and role models and those associated with forms of community service, are central for black students. Sedlacek suggests that tackling racism is multiply problematic for black students. It makes them responsible for dealing with racism; it may affect grades and whether they successfully complete courses; it is, in practice, very difficult to tackle the more covert forms of institutional racism. Black mentors provide an avenue through which discrimination can be discussed and taken back to the institution; some form of community involvement is likely to provide community support, which is usually lacking in British HEIs, where black students are often in very small minorities.

It is important that Sedlacek provides a way of addressing distinct issues that black students face which make their lives in HE very different from white students': 'For instance, many White students have self-concept problems, but these do not include the alienating effects of racism. Whites may lack a support person [or system], but the process of developing such a relationship is not the same as for Blacks because of racial and cultural variables. The researchers have demonstrated the many *unique* [my emphasis] aspects of being Black on a White campus' (Sedlacek, 1987: 490). In this context, it is worthwhile briefly referring to some difference between US and British ways of dealing with race issues at the level of policy. As Kirp (1981) suggests, the preference in race policy in Britain is for implicitness and indirection: 'Several related factors ... help to explain Britain's reliance on inexplicitness as a predicate for policy in this [race] domain: the unwillingness of Britons to perceive race as a social policy issue; a preference, in public policy, for consensual decision making; and a commitment to universalism as a public-policy norm' (p. 234).

This view is not, in fact, totally accurate. Race does sometimes become a policy issue (for example, in discussions about drugs); frequently, however, as we have seen in discussions of deracialization, it is reduced to some other issue (for example, poverty). Important points do, however, stand, in particular the implications of an emphasis of consensualism and universalism. With reference to the former, there may not, in fact, be a consensus about race issues at all, so to act consensually becomes impossible or difficult or involves support for a consensus that race is not really important. With reference to universalism, if some groups face particular problems then there may be a case for particularistic solutions to those problems.

Refocusing the issues

In the study of black access to HE and progression through HE there needs to be a reformulation of the central issues and foci. This reformulation can be indicated in the following way. There has, for a considerable time, been a stress upon *access,* upon the curriculum as *a course* and upon *quality assurance.* In addition, where these three issues have been seen as important, it is not always the case that they have been discussed with the consumer of higher education in mind. For example, much access provision, particularly in its early years, sought to feed students – often black students – into existing HE provision. What was rarely on the agenda was identifying what black students wanted from HE. What is required, therefore, is first an increasing concern with the consumer of higher education; in this case, with the black consumer. Second, there is a need for a threefold shift in emphasis: from access to *progression,* from the curriculum as a course to a concern with *the learning environment* and from quality assurance to *equality assurance.*

Taking the consumer seriously

The issue here can be put in three different, but related, ways. First, there is every reason to find out what different groups of students want, in terms of both programmes and how and where they are delivered. Second, it is important that black students have access to mainstream provision. Third, there is probably no response to the needs of black students that will not also benefit all students. We can take part-time evening delivery of programmes as an example. If black students want such delivery then a new demand has been identified and can be met. Meeting that demand has the potential to increase black students' access to mainstream provision. That new provision is likely to benefit groups of white students as well, such as mature students who work during the day.

It is, however, important to recognize that innovations in delivery and assessment (for example, modularization, APEL and CATS), will not in themselves widen access to HE, enhance progression or meet the identified needs of black students. These innovations are necessary means to enhance access, progression and quality but are not, in themselves, sufficient to achieve these ends.

From access to progression

Meeting the needs of black students in terms of access to HE is, as has been argued above, only the start of the issue. This is despite the fact that HEIs often present admissions figures for such students as evidence that they are increasingly serving the needs of diverse communities. The point of much of what has been discussed and argued throughout this book is that progression is equally, if not more, important. Part-time evening courses which recruit black and white students are no end in themselves if the black students face discrimination and isolation. Nor does any potential within HEFCE teaching quality assessment to recognize the different qualities of experience of black and white students provide any guarantee that this potential will be realized and that higher education institutions will address issues of ethnic diversity. Indeed, the relative rarity of comprehensive ethnic monitoring in HE attests to the difficulties of turning these potentials into actualities.

There is therefore a need for those who research HE, for those who teach and assess in HE and for those who measure, control and audit HE provision to refocus their concerns to issues of progression through and out of universities and colleges. Access for many groups of black students, with the possible exception of Afro-Caribbean men, has been achieved. What is less clear is whether progression through and out of HE for such students occurs in an environment of acceptance and recognition and produces degree and diploma results which are at least on a par with those for white students. The policy agenda for progression issues seems to have bypassed the issue of ethnicity and come to focus on particular quality issues: is quality uniform, is the quality of degrees declining, what is 'graduateness', why are non-completion rates rising? These issues are seen to be affecting all groups of students, and the problems of black students and how these relate to equality assurance (see below) are rarely, if ever, placed on the agenda. That the progression agenda *is* crucial is indicated, on a small, local scale, by Kibble's (n.d.) work, which shows that black students on law degree courses perform less well than white and Asian students, that they are more likely to be dissatisfied with the grading of their work and, with equal performance, that they are less likely to receive offers of articles or pupilage. These factors have to be added to factors common to many students, including financial worries and the increasing need to do part-time work while studying in HE.

From curriculum to learning environment

There is an increasing awareness that the quality of learning has to do with much more than the content and quality of courses. Put another way, the idea that the curriculum is a body of content exemplified in a course document or student handout is a far too limited one if what we are interested in is the quality of the student experience. We need to be quite explicit that the essential issue when we are looking at quality is the learning environment. This is another way of restating what was argued above: a course could be informed by issues of ethnic diversity but still exist in an environment where delivery and assessment were not appropriate to the needs of black students, and where there was discrimination and racist name calling by white students. It is in order to see whether any of these situations is occurring that comprehensive ethnic monitoring, including equal opportunities audits, is essential in HE.

From quality assurance to equality assurance

What the above points are about is, in effect, equality assurance. This is best summed up in the following:

> The three key tasks [of equality assurance] ... are as follows: (1) how to ensure high quality education for all pupils; (2) how to support the development of cultural and personal identities; (3) how to prepare pupils for full participation in society ... Such equality is not merely a matter of offering opportunities; rather, it is a matter of taking positive action to ensure that opportunities are taken up and used.
> (Runnymede Trust, 1993: 11, 12)

This comes from a text dealing with equality assurance in schools which is very specific about objectives. These are divided into: knowledge and understanding, including historical knowledge of one's own and other cultures and cultural traditions; skills, including the ability to learn from different traditions; and attitudes, including a willingness to challenge prejudice (Runnymede Trust, 1993: 13). I think that, if we replace the word 'pupil' with the word 'student' in the quotation, the points still stand. There are at least two lessons for HE in this idea of equality assurance: first, to move from a debate about simply offering opportunities and then, when people fail to take them up, arguing that 'none apply', to the idea of encouraging people, including black people, to apply; second, to provide an environment in HE for black people which validates different identities. As Phillips (1994: 79) suggests, tolerance here is not enough: 'We only tolerate what we do not like or approve of (otherwise there is no need for tolerance), and yet where difference is bound up with identity, this is hard for the tolerated to accept.'

It is interesting to look at HEFCE guidelines for the assessment of teaching quality in HE in the context of the threefold tasks set out by the Runnymede Trust. Quality assessment relates to six areas and their interrelationships: curriculum design, content and organization; teaching, learning and assessment; student progression and achievement; student support and guidance; learning resources; and quality assurance and enhancement (HEFCE, 1995: 8–9). None has priority and significant inadequacy in any one can lead to a fate similar to that which a 'failing' school will suffer under Ofsted. Two things stand out about quality assessment when looked at through the lens of equality assurance. First, and most significantly, there is nowhere any reference to the support for cultural and personal identities; as such, there is no idea of an articulation between, for example, teaching and learning or curriculum and the diversity of students, in particular ethnic diversity. Second, and related to the first point, there is a narrow understanding of the curriculum – content and structure, outcomes, opportunities for progression – which seems to preclude any linking of diversity and what is delivered. What is looked for in curriculum and teaching and learning is related to technical issues – the development of knowledge, skills, independence – which seem to operate in a vacuum and totally autonomously from any idea that different groups of students may have different needs or that some may face significant amounts of discrimination inside and outside the classroom.

We might understand this by returning to the start of this book. Not only are many academics concerned more with issues of access than with those of progression, but so, as far as black students are concerned, is HEFCE. The subtext of assessor guidelines seems to be one which sees what happens in HE as relatively neutral as far as ethnicity is concerned. This is particularly evident when we look at guidelines for classroom observation, which suggest a series of prompts (HEFCE, 1995: 27), including 'Could the member of staff be seen and heard?', 'Were the explanations clear to students?', 'Was there a variation of activity?', 'Did the member(s) of staff summarize key points and conclusions?' The vacuum here is clear and relates to the idea that content is uncontested, so that technical questions about delivery become the focus. However, as the black students in Chapters 3–6 indicate, nothing about HE is neutral with reference to ethnicity.

There is a further issue here, and that is the extent to which the rules of assessment are descriptive or prescriptive. The task of assessment is to judge academic subjects in the context of the aims and objectives of the faculties and institutions concerned. There is therefore an immediate problem where faculties make no reference to diversity of recruitment or to how this diversity is addressed in teaching and learning. In these situations there is a double absence: nothing in the guidelines for assessors on issues of ethnic diversity and nothing in the aims and objectives of particular faculties. The assessor's job therefore becomes a difficult one, which seems to have by-passed the recognition within FE that issues of ethnic diversity are relevant even in all-white colleges (FEU, 1987a, b, 1989). If we ask a simple question – 'What does an assessor do if he or she observes discrimination by staff or students in a classroom?' – the answer is unclear and the guidelines non-existent. That such a situation would be serious is clear – such discrimination reflects on teaching and learning, on management, on quality assurance systems and much else. Yet observing classes and ranking them is, as indicated above, a largely technical issue. The point is that the teaching quality assessor guidelines contain a mixture of things which look prescriptive – the development of transferable skills (HEFCE, 1995: 8–9) – and of things that are absent but, perhaps, ought to be prescriptive – that diverse students should have 'support [for] the development of cultural and personal identities' (Runnymede Trust, 1993: 11). In fact, it seems almost inconceivable that a methodology for judging teaching quality could not be prescriptive. The problem is that there are areas where there is not, but should be, prescription!

How, then, might we constructively use the HEFCE guidelines to deal with issues of equality assurance? A number of issues contained in assessment methodology could provide such a basis, including: student profiles; progression, achievement and value added; and innovation in teaching, learning and assessment. Student profiles become a basis for testing a faculty's commitment to widening access and, at some point, that profile will either confirm or deny that objective. Given a successfully widened profile, certain things will need to follow in terms of teaching, learning and assessment on the assumption that these are frequently not culturally neutral. Successfully dealing with the teaching, learning and assessment issues is likely to impact on the achievement of black students. All these, in their turn, will relate to quality assurance, resourcing and staff development. Of course, one of the difficulties here is that many of the issues of isolation, exclusion and discrimination facing black students in HE are either the brief of both HEFCE and HEQC or fall, unattended, between them.

A policy for equality

The background for any consideration of policy must be that there are two particularly significant groups within higher education: those who recognize that there is discrimination against black people but are unclear about what to do; those who, like the teachers in Gaine's (1987) study, say there is no problem here. In this final section there will be a sketch of a policy for equality as this relates to ethnic diversity. Much of this policy sketch would also relate to other groups seeking equitable treatment: women, the disabled and so on. A policy will start from the provisions of the 1976 Race Relations Act. That is its legislative basis. However, the forms of discrimination suggested by the work of Brennan and McGeevor (1987, 1990), Ohri and Shaista (1988), Jenkins (1992) and others indicates that formulating an effective policy and putting it into practice is likely to be both difficult and costly. This is why a case for an equality policy is easy to identify but difficult to operationalize. HEIs may have equality policies which aim to meet student and staff needs, enhance staff and student satisfaction, develop community links, enhance partnerships and avoid the costs of discrimination, but these policies may not work.

As a background to a policy for equality for black students and staff, it is necessary to recognize the importance of commitment and resourcing from senior management and of having such a policy as a mainstream issue. This background will form the basis for success:

> Invariably, the decision to implement positive action was taken at the highest level in the organization and continuing commitment at this level is perceived to be important to the eventual success of the initiative. There is also some evidence that employers with clear objectives (including targets) about what they want to achieve through their equal opportunities policies . . . are more likely to realize improvements in the . . . representation of ethnic minority workers.
>
> (Welsh *et al.*, 1994: summary of findings no.4)

Success in equality policy seems to be determined by a clear commitment, agreed forms of action and specified outcomes.

- *Commitment* will be evidenced by a number of factors, including: written policies which are tied to strategic planning; person or persons with overall management responsibility; action planning which relates to resourcing, outcomes and targets, roles and responsibilities of senior management, structures for internal and external consultation. In addition, commitment will be evidenced by awareness of the policy and its related practices among not only staff and students, but also local communities and other customers.
- Policy will require a range of *actions*, both internal and external. The former will include gathering of data on applications, admissions, retention, achievement and progression; the setting of targets for recruitment, locally, regionally and nationally; staff training; auditing of provision; the establishment of grievance procedures. External actions will include widespread consultations with local communities, marketing, where necessary in community languages, monitoring of any placements and responding to advice from external agencies.
- *Outcomes* and related performance indicators will include: a fair representation of minority ethnic groups; high student retention rates; increased representation from local black communities; few grievances and complaints; a good understanding of policy among staff and students; good progression to the next stage in the system.

Finally, we can quote from some significantly wise words addressed to administrators in US universities which are relevant to the UK:

> Every institution of higher education worthy of its designation as a college or university should measure up to high standards of ethnic sensitivity and racial civility. All colleges and universities should be committed to engendering values and implementing policies that will enhance respect for individuals and their cultures with an acceptance of the premise that the nation's cultural, racial and ethnic diversity . . . is one of the most valued, significant and important characteristics of . . . democracy . . . In the quest for equity in higher education, administrators [and teachers] must recognise that understanding is a condition of, not a synonym for, solutions.
>
> (H. Scott, 1990: 73)

Bibliography

Abramson, M., Bird, J. and Stennett, A. (eds) (1996) *Further and Higher Education Partnerships: the Future for Collaboration*. Buckingham, SRHE/Open University Press.

Allan, C. (1992) Widening participation in HE; a PCFC perspective, *Journal of Access Studies*, 7(1), 33–41.

Anthias, F. and Yuval-Davis, N. (1992) *Racialized Boundaries*. London, Routledge.

Astin, A. W. (1982) *Minorities in American Higher Education: Recent Trends, Current Prospects and Recommendations*. San Francisco, Jossey-Bass.

Atkinson, P. (1990) *The Ethnographic Imagination: the Politics and Poetics of Ethnography*. London, Routledge.

Barker, M. (1981) *The New Racism*. London, Junction Books.

Baxter, A. and Glasner, P. (1986) *What Young People Think*. Bristol, Bristol Polytechnic Department of Economics and Social Science.

Bhat, A., Carr-Hill, R. and Ohri, S. (eds) (1988) *Britain's Black Population*. London, Gower.

Bigger, S. (1996) Post-16 Compact in Birmingham: school and college links with higher education. In M. Abramson, J. Bird and A. Stennett (eds) *Further and Higher Education Partnerships: the Future for Collaboration*. Buckingham, SRHE/Open University Press.

Billig, M., Condor, S., Edwards, D., Gane, M., Middleton, D. and Radley, A. (1988) *Ideological Dilemmas*. London, Sage.

Billingham, S. (1988) *Ethnic Monitoring in Higher Education*. Conference report, Preston, Lancashire Polytechnic Race Equality Unit.

Bird, J., Crawley, G. and Shebani, A. (1993) *Franchising and Access to Higher Education*. Bristol, University of the West of England/Employment Department.

Bird, J., Myler, A. and Yee, W. (1992a) *Widening Access to Higher Education for Black People*. Bristol, University of the West of England/Employment Department.

Bird, J., Shebani, A. and Francombe, D. (1992b) *Ethnic Monitoring and Admissions to Higher Education*. Bristol, University of the West of England/Employment Department.

Bird, J. and Yee, W. C. (1994) *From Compacts to Consortia: a Study of Partnerships Involving Schools, Colleges and HEIs*. Bristol, University of the West of England/Employment Department/UCAS.

Bird, J., Yee, W. and Myler, A. (1992c) Rhetorics of access, realities of exclusion, *Journal of Access Studies*, 7(2), 147–63.

Booth, H. (1988) Identifying ethnic origin: the past, present and future of official data production. In A. Bhat, R. Carr-Hill and S. Ohri (eds) *Britain's Black Population*. London, Gower.

Braham, P., Rattansi, A. and Skellington, R. (1992) *Racism and Antiracism: Inequalities, Opportunities and Policies*. London, Sage.

Brennan, J. and Jarry, D. (1991) *Degrees of Inequality*. London, Jessica Kingsley.

Brennan, J. and McGeevor, P. (1987) *The Employment of Graduates from Ethnic Minorities*. London, Commission for Racial Equality.

Brennan, J. and McGeevor, P. (1990) *Ethnic Minorities and the Graduate Labour Market*. London, Commission for Racial Equality.

Brienberg, P. (1987) The black perspective in higher education, *Multicultural Teaching*, 6(1), 36–8.

Brown, H. and Sommerlad, E. (1992) Staff development in higher education: towards a learning organisation?, *Higher Education Quarterly*, 46(2), 174–90.

Burrell, L. F. (1980) Is there a future for Black students on predominantly White campuses?, *Integrateducation*, 18(4), 23–7.

Cashmore, E. and Troyna, B. (1988) *Introduction to Race Relations*. London, Routledge.

Chevannes, M. and Reeves, F. (1987) The black voluntary school movement: definition, context and prospects. In B. Troyna (ed.), *Racial Inequality in Education*. London, Tavistock.

Clough, E. and Drew, D. (1985) *Futures in Black and White*. London, Pavic Publications.

Cohen, P. and Rattansi, A. (1991) *Rethinking Racism and Antiracism*. London, Runnymede Trust.

Cole, M. (1993) 'Black and ethnic minority' or 'Asian, black and other minority ethnic': a further note on nomenclature, *Sociology*, 27(4), 671–3.

Coleman, D. and Salt, J. (1992) *The British Population*. Oxford, Oxford University Press.

Connolly, C. (1994) Shades of discrimination: university entry data 1900–92. In S. Haselgrove (ed.) *The Student Experience*. Buckingham, SRHE/Open University Press.

Craft, A. and Craft, M. (1983) The participation of ethnic minorities in further and higher education, *Educational Research*, 21(1), 10–19.

CRE (1980) *Why Keep Ethnic Records?* London, CRE.

CRE (1989a) *Racial Discrimination: a Guide to the Race Relations Act of 1976*. London, CRE.

CRE (1989b) *Code of Practice for the Elimination of Racial Discrimination in Education*. London, CRE.

Demaine, J. (1989) Race, categorisation and educational achievement, *British Journal of the Sociology of Education*, 10(2), 195–214.

Demaine, J. (1993) Racism, ideology and education: the last word on the Honeyford affair?, *British Journal of the Sociology of Education*, 14(4), 409–14.

Dorn, A. (1991) Notes on ethnic minority participation in HE. Unpublished paper presented to the Polytechnics and Colleges Funding Council Conference on Widening Participation in HE, London.

Eggleston, J. (1993) The post-sixteen education of young black Britons. In A. Fyfe and P. Figueroa (eds) *Education for Cultural Diversity*. London, Routledge.

Farish, M., McPake, J., Powney, J. and Weiner, G. (1995). *Equal Opportunities in College and Universities: Towards Better Practice*. Buckingham, SRHE/Open University Press.

FEFC (1995) *Community Colleges in the USA*. Coventry, FEFC.

FEU (1985) *Curricular Strategies for Disadvantaged Adults.* London, FEU.
FEU (1986a) *Anti-racist Curriculum Review and Staff Development.* London, FEU.
FEU (1986b) *The Experience of Black Students in FE.* London, FEU.
FEU (1986c) *Towards a Non-racist Curriculum.* London, FEU.
FEU (1986d) *Black Images in the 16–19 Curriculum.* London, FEU.
FEU (1987a) *Mainstream Curricula in a Multicultural Society.* London, FEU.
FEU (1987b) *FE in Black and White.* London, FEU.
FEU (1989) *Staff Development for a Multicultural Society.* London, FEU.
FEU/FEDA (1995) *Community Profiling.* London, Further Education Development Agency.
FEU/REPLAN (1989) *The Outreach College.* London, FEU.
Foster, P. (1990) *Policy and Practice in Multicultural Education.* London, Routledge.
Gaine, C. (1987) *No Problem Here: a Practical Guide to Education and 'Race' in White Schools.* London, Hutchinson.
Gibbon, P. (1992) Equal opportunities policy and race equality. In P. Braham, A. Rattansi and R. Skellington (eds) *Racism and Antiracism,* London, Sage.
Giddens, A. (1989) *Sociology.* Cambridge, Polity Press.
Gillborn, D. (1990) *'Race', Ethnicity and Education: Teaching and Learning in Multiethnic Schools.* London, Unwin Hyman.
Gillborn, D. (1995) *Racism and Antiracism in Real Schools.* Buckingham, Open University Press.
Gilroy, P. (1981) You can't fool the youths . . . race and class formation in the 1980s, *Race and Class,* 23(2/3), 207–22.
Gilroy, P. (1987) *There Ain't No Black in the Union Jack.* London, Hutchinson.
Gilroy, P. (1993) *Small Acts.* London: Serpent's Tail.
Gilroy, P. (1994) *Black Atlantic: Modernity and Double Consciousness.* London, Verso Press.
Gordon, C. (1980) *Michel Foucault: Power/Knowledge.* New York, Pantheon.
Gordon, P. (1992) The racialization of statistics. In P. Skellington and P. Morris (eds) *'Race' in Britain Today,* London, Sage.
Hage, G. (1994) Locating multiculturalism's other: a critique of practical tolerance, *New Formations,* 24 (Winter), 19–34.
Haselgrove, S. (ed.) (1994) *The Student Experience.* Buckingham, SRHE/Open University Press.
Hammersley, M. (1992) *What's Wrong with Ethnography.* London, Routledge.
HEFCE (1995) *Assessors' Handbook.* Bristol, HEFCE.
Hubbock, J. and Carter, S. (1980) *Half a Chance? A Report on Job Discrimination among Young Blacks in Nottingham.* Nottingham CRE.
James, A. and Jeffcoate, R. (1981) *The School in a Multicultural Society.* London, Harper Row.
Jenkins, R. (1986) *Racism and Recruitment: Managers, Organisations and Equal Opportunity in the Labour Market.* Cambridge, Cambridge University Press.
Jenkins, R. (1992) Black workers in the labour market: the price of recession. In P. Braham *et al.* (eds) *Racism and Anti-racism: Inequalities, Opportunities and Policies.* London, Sage/The Open University.
Jewson, N., Mason, D., Bowen, R., Mulvaney, K. and Parmar, S. (1991) Universities and ethnic minorities: the public face, *New Community,* 17(2), 183–99.
Jewson, N., Mason, D., Drewett, A. and Rossiter, W. (1995) *Formal Equal Opportunities Policies and Employment Best Practice.* London, Department for Education and Employment.

Jones, T. (1993) *Britain's Ethnic Minorities.* London, PSI.

Jordan, S. and Yeomans, D. (1995) Critical ethnography: problems in contemporary theory and practice, *British Journal of the Sociology of Education,* 16(3), 389–408.

Jowell, R. and Witherspoon, S. (annually) *British Social Attitudes.* London, Gower and Social and Community Planning Research.

Kazantzis, M., Cope, B., Noble, G. and Poynting, S. (1994) *Culture of Schooling: Pedagogies of Cultural Difference and Social Access.* London, Falmer Press.

Kibble, N. (n.d.) *The Performance of Non-traditional Students on Law Degrees and on the Professional Courses.* London, South Bank Polytechnic.

Kirp, D. L. (1981) Inexplicitness as racial policy in Britain and the US. In A. Yarmolinski, L. Leibman and C. Schelling (eds) *Race and Schooling in the City.* New York, Harvard University Press.

Leicester, M. and Taylor, M. (1992) *Ethnicity and Education.* London, Kogan Page.

Leicester, M. (1993a) *Race for a Change in Continuing and Higher Education.* Buckingham, SRHE/Open University Press.

Leicester, M. (1993b) Anti-racist access, *Journal of Access Studies,* 8(3), 220–4.

Lyon, S. (1988) Unequal opportunities: black minorities and access to higher education, *Journal of Further and Higher Education,* 12(3), 21–37.

McCarthy, C. (1990) *Race and Curriculum: Social Inequality and the Theories and Politics of Difference in Contemporary Research on Schooling.* London, Falmer Press.

McCarthy, C. (1994) The politics of culture: multicultural education after the content debate, *Discourse,* 14(2), 1–16.

Matheu, L. (1995) *Social Movements and Social Classes.* London, Sage.

Mason, D. (1994) On the dangers of disconnecting race and racism, *Sociology,* 28(4), 845–58.

Melucci, A. (1989) *Nomads of the Present: Social Movements and Individual Needs in Contemporary Society.* London, Hutchinson.

Mendus, A. (1989) *Toleration and the Limits of Liberalism.* London, Macmillan.

Miles, R. (1989) *Racism.* London, Routledge.

Miles, R. (1993) *Racism after 'Race Relations'.* London, Routledge.

Mills, C. W. (1970) *The Sociological Imagination.* London, Penguin.

Modood, T. (1993) Subtle shades of student distinction, *The Times Higher Education Supplement,* 16 July, iv.

Modood, T. (1994) Political blackness and British Asians, *Sociology,* 28(4), 859–76.

Modood, T. and Shiner, M. (1994) *Ethnic Minorities and Higher Education.* London, PSI.

Moodley, R. (ed.) (1995) *Education for Transformation: Black Access to Higher Education.* Leeds, Thomas Danby Publications.

Mortimore, P., Sammons, P., Stoll, L., Lewis, D. and Ecob, R. (1988) *School Matters: the Junior Years.* Wells, Open Books.

Ofsted (1994) *Framework for the Inspection of Schools.* London, Ofsted.

Ohri, S. (1988) The politics of racism, statistics and equal opportunity: towards a black perspective. In A. Bhat, R. Carr-Hill and S. Ohri (eds) *Britain's Black Population.* London: Gower.

Ohri, S. and Shaista, S. (1988) Race, employment and unemployment. In A. Bhat *et al.* (eds) *Britain's Black Population.* London, Gower.

Owen, D. (1992) *Ethnic Minorities in Britain: Settlement Patterns.* Census Statistical Paper no. 1, University of Warwick Centre for Research in Ethnic Relations.

PCFC (1992) *Widening Participation in Higher Education.* London, PCFC.

Paul, E., Miller, F., Paul, J. and Ahrens, J. (1987) *Equal Opportunity.* Oxford, Blackwell.

Phillips, A. (1994) Dealing with difference: a politics of ideas or a politics of presence, *Constellations*, 1(1), 74–91.

Prentice Baptiste, H., Waxman, H., Walker de Felix, J. and Anderson, J. (1990) *Leadership, Equity and School Effectiveness*. London, Sage.

Race Relations Employment Advisory Service (RREAS) (1991) *Equal Opportunities: What Is Positive Action?* Sheffield, Employment Department.

Rattansi, A. (1992) Changing the subject: racism, culture and education. In J. Donald and A. Rattansi (eds) *'Race', Culture and Difference*. London, Sage.

REPLAN/NIACE (1990) *Education Guidance with Black Communities*. Leicester, NIACE.

Rhodes, P. J. (1994) Race-of-interviewer effects: a brief comment, *Sociology*, 28(2), 527–58.

Ross, K. (1990) Eight myths about minorities in higher education, *The College Board Review*, 155, 12–19 and 45–7.

Runnymede Trust (1993) *Equality Assurance in Schools*. London, Trentham Books.

Said, E. (1978) *Orientalism*. London, Routledge.

Sammons, P., Hillman, J. and Mortimore, P. (1995) *Key Characteristics of Effective Schools: a Review of School Effectiveness Research*. London, Ofsted and University of London Institute of Education.

Sammons, P. and Newbury, K. (1989) *Ethnic Monitoring in Further and Higher Education*. London, ILEA.

Sandal, K. (1986) Michel Foucault: intellectual work and politics, *Telos*, 67 (Spring), 121–34.

Sarup, M. (1986) *The Politics of Multi-racial Education*. London, Routledge.

Scott, A. (1990) *Ideology and the New Social Movements*. London, Unwin Hyman.

Scott, H. (1990) The quest for equity: imperatives for administrators in higher education. In H. Prentice Baptiste, H. Waxman, J. Walker de Felix and J. Anderson (eds) *Leadership, Equity and School Effectiveness*. London, Sage.

Sedlacek, W. E. (1987) Black students in white campuses: 20 years of research, *Journal of College Student Personnel*, 28, 484–95.

Sedlacek, W. E., Lewis, J. A. and Brooks, G. C. (1974) Black and other minority admissions to large universities: a four year survey of policies and outcomes, *Research in Higher Education*, 2, 221–30.

Sedlacek, W. E. and Webster, D. W. (1978) Admission and retention of minority students in large universities, *Journal of College Student Personnel*, 19, 242–8.

Showunmi, V. and Constantine-Simms, D. (1995) *Teacher for the Future*. London, Trentham Books.

Silverman, D. (1993) *Interpreting Qualitative Data*. London, Sage.

Simmons-Bird, M. (1992) *Name Calling and Bullying in Avon Schools: a Discussion Paper*. Bristol, Avon TVEI (unpublished).

Singh, R. (1990) Ethnic minority experience in higher education, *Higher Education Quarterly*, 44(4), 344–59.

Sivanandan, A. (1985) RAT and the degradation of black struggle, *Race and Class*, 26(4), 1–33.

Skellington, P. and Morris, P. (1992) *'Race' in Britain Today*. London, Sage.

Smith, A. M. (1994) *New Right Discourses on Race and Sexuality*. Cambridge, Cambridge University Press.

Solomos, J. and Back, L. (1995) *Race, Politics and Social Change*. London, Routledge.

Stone, M. (1980) *The Education of the Black Child in Britain*. London, Fontana.

Taylor, C. A. (1986) Black students on predominantly white college campuses, *Journal of College Student Personnel*, 27, 196–202.

Taylor, C. and Gutmann, A. (1992) *Multiculturalism and 'the Politics of Recognition'*. Princeton, NJ, Princeton University Press.

Taylor, P. (1992) Ethnic group data and applications to HE, *Higher Education Quarterly*, 46(4), 359–74.

Tizard, B., Blatchford, P., Burke, J., Farquhar, C. and Plewis, I. (1988) *Young Children at School in the Inner City*. Hove, Laurence Erlbaum.

Tomlinson, S. (1983) Black women in higher education – case studies of university women in Britain. In L. Barton and S. Walker (eds) *Race, Class and Education*. London, Croom Helm.

Troyna, B. (1984) Fact or artefact: the 'educational underachievement' of black pupils, *British Journal of Sociology of Education*, 5(2), 153–66.

Troyna, B. (1987) *Racial Inequalities in Education*. London, Tavistock.

Troyna, B. (1993) *Racism and Education*. Buckingham, Open University Press.

Troyna, B. and Carrington, B. (1990) *Education, Racism and Reform*. London, Routledge.

UCAS (1994) *Statistical Supplements to the PCAS Annual Report, 1992–1993, Incorporating Time-series of PCAS Statistics, 1986–1993*. Cheltenham, UCAS.

UCAS (1995) *Annual Report, 1993–94 Entry*. London, UCAS.

UCCA (1992) *Statistical Supplement to the Twenty Ninth Report, 1990–1991*. Cheltenham, UCCA.

UDACE (1990) *Black Community Access: a Development Paper*. London, NIACE.

Van Dijk, T. (1993) *Elite Discourse and Racism*. London, Sage.

Welsh, C., Knox, J. and Brett, M. (1994) *Acting Positively: Positive Action under the Race Relations Act 1976*. Sheffield, Capita Management Consultancy for the Employment Department.

Westwood, S. (1992) Power/knowledge: the politics of transformative research, *Studies in the Education of Adults*, 24(2), 191–8.

Williams, J., Cocking, J. and Davies, L. (1989) *Words or Deeds: a Review of Equal Opportunity Policies in Higher Education*. London, Commission for Racial Equality.

Williams, L. (1988) *Partial Surrender: Race and Resistance in Youth Work*. Lewes, Falmer Press.

Wright, C. (1987) Black students – white teachers. In B. Troyna (ed.) *Racial Inequality in Education*. London, Tavistock.

Index

The Society for Research into Higher Education

The Society for Research into Higher Education exists to stimulate and coordinate research into all aspects of higher education. It aims to improve the quality of higher education through the encouragement of debate and publication on issues of policy, on the organization and management of higher education institutions, and on the curriculum and teaching methods.

The Society's income is derived from subscriptions, sales of its books and journals, conference fees and grants. It receives no subsidies, and is wholly independent. Its individual members include teachers, researchers, managers and students. Its corporate members are institutions of higher education, research institutes, professional, industrial and governmental bodies. Members are not only from the UK, but from elsewhere in Europe, from America, Canada and Australasia, and it regards its international work as among its most important activities.

Under the imprint *SRHE & Open University Press*, the Society is a specialist publisher of research, having some 60 titles in print. The Editorial Board of the Society's Imprint seeks authoritative research or study in the above fields. It offers competitive royalties, a highly recognizable format in both hardback and paperback and the worldwide reputation of the Open University Press.

The Society also publishes *Studies in Higher Education* (three times a year), which is mainly concerned with academic issues, *Higher Education Quarterly* (formerly *Universities Quarterly*), mainly concerned with policy issues, *Research into Higher Education Abstracts* (three times a year), and *SRHE News* (four times a year).

The Society holds a major annual conference in December, jointly with an institution of higher education. In 1993, the topic was 'Governments and the Higher Education Curriculum: Evolving Partnerships' at the University of Sussex in Brighton. In 1994, it was 'The Student Experience' at the University of York and in 1995, 'The Changing University' at Heriot-Watt University in Edinburgh. Conferences in 1996 include 'Working in Higher Education' at Cardiff Institute of Higher Education.

The Society's committees, study groups and branches are run by the members. The groups at present include:

Teacher Education Study Group
Continuing Education Group
Staff Development Group
Excellence in Teaching and Learning

Benefits to members

Individual

Individual members receive:

- SRHE: News, the Society's publications list, conference details and other material included in mailings.
- Greatly reduced rates for *Studies in Higher Education* and *Higher Education Quarterly.*
- A 35 per cent discount on all **SRHE & Open University Press** publications.
- Free copies of the Proceedings – commissioned papers on the theme of the Annual Conference.
- Free copies of *Research into Higher Education Abstracts.*
- Reduced rates for conferences.
- Extensive contacts and scope for facilitating initiatives.
- Reduced reciprocal memberships.
- Free copies of the *Register of Members' Research Interests.*

Corporate

Corporate members receive:

- All benefits of individual members, plus
- Free copies of *Studies in Higher Education.*
- Unlimited copies of the Society's publications at reduced rates.
- Special rates for its members e.g. to the Annual Conference.
- The right to submit application for the Society's research grants.

Membership details: SRHE, 3 Devonshire Street, London WIN 2BA, UK. Tel: 0171 637 2766. Fax: 0171 637 2781
Catalogue: SRHE & Open University Press, Celtic Court, 22 Ballmoor, Buckingham MK18 1XW. Tel: (01280) 823388.

EQUAL OPPORTUNITIES IN COLLEGES AND UNIVERSITIES
TOWARDS BETTER PRACTICES

Maureen Farish, Joanna McPake, Janet Powney and Gaby Weiner

This book is the *first* attempt to consider the effectiveness of equal opportunities policies for staff (in colleges and universities) after the policies have been passed and implemented. It suggests future strategies for policy-makers and equal opportunities 'activists' in the light of the findings which concern structure, policy coherence and policy contradiction.

It provides an account, through the detailed case-studies of three educational institutions (one further education college, one 'new' and one 'old' university) of how equal opportunities policy-making has developed over the last decade and what gains have been made. It also examines the complexity of trying to judge the effectiveness of such policies by viewing policy from a number of standpoints including those of managers and policy-makers, those charged with implementing the policies (for instance, equal opportunities or women's officers), and those at the receiving end. In trying to unravel the complexity, what emerges is the importance of institutional history and context as well as policy structure and content.

Contents
Setting the context of equal opportunities in educational organizations – Borough college incorporated: case study – Town university: case study – Metropolitan university: case study – Critical moments and illuminative insights – Codifying policy and practice – Contrasting contexts – Shared themes – Munro bagging: towards better practices – Appendix: research methodology – Bibliography – Index.

224pp   0 335 19416 8 (Paperback)   0 335 19417 6 (Hardback)

RACE FOR A CHANGE IN CONTINUING AND HIGHER EDUCATION

Mal Leicester

Mal Leicester argues that an antiracist, pluralist approach can transform adult education in higher education and in other contexts; that adult and continuing education departments are potential agents of change in higher education with regard to the development of antiracist higher education; and that race and culture issues, properly understood, could empower higher education in its most central tasks. She justifies these claims by focusing on both theoretical debates and practical experience (drawing on her own and others' empirical research).

Race for a Change in Continuing and Higher Education will stimulate thinking on theoretical considerations, and offers guidance for practice both in terms of student learning and of securing relevant institutional change.

Contents

Part 1: Antiracist continuing education: agent and model – Continuing education as change agent: inreach and outreach – Conceptual clarification: 'racism' and 'antiracist education' – Conceptual clarification: 'antiracist continuing education' – Practising what we preach: departmental change – Change agents and models: a UCACE survey revisited – Part 2: Continuing antiracist education: the university transformed – Coming of age: the mature university – Outreach: antiracist access – Access and maintaining academic standards – Inreach: accessibility and the antiracist university – Higher education for all – Appendix – Bibliography – Index.

160pp   0 335 09767 7 (Paperback)   0 335 09768 5 (Hardback)